First published in 2014 by Doggerel Delights, with the design, illustrations and typeset by
Monica Conaghan.
This second edition published in 2016 by Barrallier Books Pty. Ltd trading as Echo Books

Registered Office: 35-37 Gordon Avenue, West Geelong, Victoria 3220, Australia.

www.echobooks.com.au

National Library of Australia Cataloguing-in-Publication entry.

Creator: Walker, John, 1947-, author.

Title: The loaded doggerel : reflections of a ten pound pom forty years on/ John Walker;
Monica Conaghan, illustrator.
Edition: Second edition.
ISBN: 9780994577849 (paperback)
Subjects: Australian poetry.
Other Creators/Contributors: Conaghan, Monica, illustrator.
Dewey Number: A821.4

Book layout and design by Peter Gamble, Canberra.
Set in Garamond Premier Pro Light Display, 12/17 and Aquiline Two

Written by John Walker—john.walker@ozemail.com.au
Illustrated By MRC Designs 0415502872.

www.echobooks.com.au

The Loaded Doggerel

John Walker

with
Illustrations by
Monica Conaghan

Introducing the Authors

In 'real' life, John Walker is a criminologist, based in Queanbeyan, near Canberra, Australia. He is actively involved in a range of sports, although mainly as an administrator or spectator rather than a competitor these days. He is also an enthusiastic fan of a range of music styles, mostly from the jazz and swing genres. Writing poetry, along with learning to play the clarinet, started as a 'pre-retirement' activity:– preparing for life after work, and keeping the brain cells active. It soon became a rather good way of passing the time on long air journeys or while waiting for inspiration on a work project. One evening in 2012, he wandered, feeling *lonely as a cloud*, into a monthly meeting of the Queanbeyan Bush Poets, ready to face the music. Were his efforts *real* poetry? Their encouragement that night, and ever since, has resulted in this book.

Monica Conaghan, a Creative all rounder spends far too much time pondering and visualising, who gets excited over a the way piece of wood is decaying, and brings together associations, that leave others scratching their heads, until she explains how the idea came about, often leaving the listener astonished and amazed at her ability to draw on many parts of life to create unique and timeless designs, illustrations, & ideas.

A creative entrepreneur, that dreams in ideas as she sleeps, and wakes up and has to write it down immediately, recently turning away from the computer and going back to where it all started creating by hand ... Inspired by history, nature, and quirkiness. Monica hopes you enjoy this book as much as she has contributing to it!

Acknowledgements

I would first like to thank all those who have encouraged me in poetry, in particular, the members of the Queanbeyan Bush Poets, led by Laurie McDonald, whose monthly meetings have been my sounding board. And Lucy Nesci, organiser of the Cooma Feast of Poetry, who convinced me to enter some of my work in the 2012 Poetry Competition. A 'Highly Commended' at one's first attempt is a real confidence booster!

I should also thank my wife Karan, who has had to put up with me frequently waking up in the middle of the night with a desperate urge to write some idea down before I forgot it, and helping me develop all sorts of unlikely scenarios!

Thanks also to Monica Conaghan for her wonderful illustrations and her help in putting all this together!

Finally, I would like to acknowledge the reference to Henry Lawson, whose *Loaded Dog* opened my eyes to the wonderful heritage of Australian writing.

John Walker
October 2015

Contents

The Arts

Starting out as a 'novice', and finding your way amongst the artistic fraternity can be a bit daunting, and this section includes some thoughts on issues arising on John's personal journey.

The 2-Plated Poet

Is doggerel in the ear of the beholder?
And is poetry a 'better' kind of verse?
Are television jingles just like Shakespeare
Or a sign that modern culture's getting worse?

Am I only wasting time composing rubbish,
Or will 'real' poets recognise my worth?
Will they hang on every word as I recite it,
Or just roll around in unconcealed mirth?

I stand before you now, a trembling mortal
On judgement day—which way the verdict goes?
Is poetry an art I can aspire to,
Or should I really leave it to the prose?

A radio programme poet declared that 'orange' was one
word in the English language that didn't rhyme
with anything else.
Rubbish, I said to myself ...

The Orange

The soft, round fruit we call an orange
Was first discovered by a foreign
Gentleman, who walked his dog
Around some prehistoric bog

Nowadays, for just a florin,
Jam is made from tons of orange.
Countries round the world all trade
In various forms of Marmalade.

While Scotsmen kept through ancient history
The contents of their kilt a mystery,
It's common knowledge they keep an orange
Tucked up carefully in their sporran.
Generally they last for weeks
(and taste much better than sprouts or leeks).

The English tongue is very strange,
It has no words to rhyme orange.
So if these verses make you cringe,
You try to make one rhyme orange !

*Here's true story, from my youth ... I sat in my room and
watched a most magnificent 'penumbral eclipse' of the moon...*

I Watched the Moon

I watched the moon turn rusty brown one night when I was young
It really was a wondrous sight, but something there was wrong.
The scientific reason for it all's not hard to see
But that is not the problem that is really bothering me.

The Earth gets in the way of light, in passing from the sun.
And casts a sunset shadow on the full face of the moon.
It's beautiful—I must admit—but something lacks for me.
There ought to be some sound effects to go with what we see.

Au Clair de Lune (Debussy) is a bit too light, I know.
And Beethoven's Sonata is OK, but just too slow.
Blue Moon is just plain wrong, but such a lovely song, it's true.
And Bad Moon Rising hasn't got the credence that is due.

Turn Rusty Brown

Glenn Miller's Moonlight Serenade's OK, but it's too short.
And Benny Goodman's Moonglow is a classic last resort.
I'd love to 'Fly me to the Moon'—see what it's like from there,
But jazz is not the mood we need to match this grand affair.

The very least, for sights like this, is Gustav Holst or Grieg.
And Thus Spake Zarathrustra is almost in their league.
But, to my mind, the only tune these noble scenes evoke
Is Edward Elgar's finest—an orchestral masterstroke!

The moon's an enigmatic thing—that's never been in doubt.
Its variations night by night took years to figure out.
But this eclipse's visuals need a sound track that inspires,
And Edward Elgar's Nimrod is the tune that it requires.

This one is a genuine cri-de-coeur, *based on countless hours trying to make sense of a system that lacks any logic! The best music lesson I can remember was delivered, in a Paris cafe by a French mathematics student in clear and concise calculus—in French!*

Did you Learn to Read Music?

Did you learn to read music? Those symbols are meant
To convey to us all the composers intent.
To let us know just how he/she would have said
His/her piece of music's supposed to be played.

Modern music notation's been out there for yonks,
Developed, they say, by Italian monks.
But when you look closely, you'd have to confess
That the scheme they came up with's a terrible mess.

The twelve notes they gave alphabetical names,
From A up to G—but that's seven, you exclaim!
Then they called them an octave, which doesn't relate—
Even my grasp of Latin tells me that means eight!

Their knowledge of maths was a REALLY bad dream,
As a fifth plus a third makes a whole in their scheme.
And a three over four, while the maths is quite false,
Can be read—so they said - as an invite to waltz.

With quavers and crotchets and minims and breves,
The lengths of the notes also beg to deceive!
The breve is the longest, with logic quite fraught,
Since breve is pure Latin - its meaning is 'short'.

They write all these notes on a staff with five lines,
And with strange exhortations like 'DC al fine's.
And a really low 'C' on a line they will place,
But the next higher 'C' you will find in a space.

And these inconsistencies are not alone
As each different instrument's got its own tone.
Your clarinet 'C' is in fact a flat 'B',
But a French Horn blows 'F' when you think it's a 'C'.

No wonder it's so hard for people like me,
To become the musician that they'd like to be!
I can play it by ear, on a good day, with ease,
But the written stuff might as well be in Chinese!

This one's a bit naughty, so if you're of a nervous disposition, please turn your eyes away when you read it. Apologies to André Rieux, who doesn't really have an 'a' in his surname, but it rhymes better with one.

The Naked Poet

Have you noticed there's one way to guarantee
That your work will be famous, and you'll be on TV?
Whatever you do, if you're wanting a mention,
You have to be nude to attract their attention.

There's 'How to Look Good' and the Naked News,
Then the Naked Chef, in your TV views.
The Naked Planet, and the Naked City.
There's surely a trend here—and more's the pity!

But, 'can't beat 'em, join 'em', makes sense in this age,
From now on stark naked I'll be on the stage.
My cov'rage I'll shed, in one sense, to ensure
More cov'rage—in the other sense—than ever before.

If these tactics work, my poems'll become
As familiar a sight on TV as my bum!
I'll soon be as famous as André Rieaux
And have millions of viewers tune into my show.

The sales of my poetry no doubt will soar,
And no longer will people describe me as poor!
Live sessions will be absolutely the best
With even the dress circle being undressed!

It seems so attractive, but do I really dare
Get up on a stage with my body so bare?
Is it too much to ask for pursuing my arts
To display all the details of my private parts?

Oh, what the heck—poets like Coleridge and Keats
Were so bloody poor that they died in the streets.
Well, I'm not having that, and don't care if it's rude,
So why shouldn't a poet perform in the nude?

My 'poems' come to me at all hours of the day, and no matter what I happen to be doing at the time. Is it a blessing or a curse?

What Does a Poet Do in his Spare Time?

What on earth does a poet do in his spare time?
Does he just close his mind to the quest for a rhyme?
Can he walk through the shops without noticing where,
The chips and the dips are co-located there?

Can he jump in his car without wondering what'l
Provide him with something that's rhyming with throttle?
Can he polish it up without writing a sonnet
Or two on the hue of his pride-and-joy's bonnet?

Can he walk through the bush without seeing a roo,
And link it in rhyme to a white cockatoo?
Can he gaze at a wattle with never a curse
That he should've used that in the previous verse?

Can he go down the pub and partake of the booze
Without ever a thought of the brain cells he'll lose?
Does each meal at a bistro turn out a disaster
As his mind just works faster while eating his pasta?

Do all thoughts of his boss bring to mind a 'dead loss'?
If he ever found out it could make him quite cross!
Poets' minds are a minefield of tricks such as these,
Is it a skill or a mental disease?

Are these brains of ours special, with skills that the rest
Of humanity lacks—so that ours are the best?
Or is it a curse till the day that we drop?
I hate it! I hate it! I just cannot stop!

Possibly a true story. The first few verses definitely sound familiar. I'll let you know about the rest, as time goes by ...

Late-Onset Clarinet

I'm going to learn the clarinet, though it's fairly late in life.
I tried to learn the thing before, but it only brought me strife.
It squawked and squeaked and woke the kids, when fast asleep at night,
So forty years it lay there, in the cupboard, out of sight.

I'm going to learn the clarinet, though it's going to be quite hard.
I want to play Mood Indigo just like Barney Bigard.
He co-wrote it with Ellington, and played it with the band.
But how he made it sound like that, I'll never understand!!

I'm going to play the clarinet, as good as Acker Bilk,
And get those mellow tones just right, like others of his ilk.
I'll find some lonely beach retreat, and practice till it's right,
Not just a Stranger on the Shore, but 'Starring Here' tonight!

I'm going to learn the clarinet, and Stomp at the Savoy,
So Benny Goodman's legacy remains to be enjoyed.
And Sidney Bechet's Petite Fleur is one I'll try to play.
You'll see me at the Albert Hall, for certainty, one day!

I'm going to learn the clarinet - at my age you ask why?
I figure that an old folks home's a boring place to die.
I plan to really stir them up, before I go from there,
And play my favourites all day long from my old rockin' chair!

I'm going to learn the clarinet, come back to haunt the joint.
Get rid of all that Kenny G—it's Muzak—what's the point!
My songs instead will thrill the folks—while waiting to check out!
They'll talk about ME when I've gone—of that there'll be no doubt!

And if, right at the Pearly Gates, St Peter lets me through,
I'll have my clarinet on hand, 'cause I'm going to play there too!
But if the guy in charge up there just won't let me perform,
I'll go down to the other place - play hot jazz in the warm!

Statisticians only get things right about half the time ...

The Chimpanzee and the Typewriter

There was a theory, years ago, that, given enough time,
A chimpanzee with a typewriter would type out Shakespeare's rhymes.
The statisticians worked it out, and so it must be true,
But typewriters are now so scarce, what's a chimpanzee to do?

But zoos around the world then all decided to invest
In laptops for each chimpanzee to accelerate the quest.
The expectation was that they'd use Publisher or Word,
But sad to say those hopes were dashed! This is what occurred.

No sooner were those chimps logged in they're surfing on the net.
Despite all these resources, not a single chimp has yet
Come up with some Shakespearean words, or even some Pam Ayres.
They have, however, had some quite spectacular success.

A monkey based in Lagos Zoo earned very large amounts,
Through emails sent solicitating people's bank accounts.
The gullible around the world got more than just a glimpse
Of how much can be stolen by an enterprising chimp.

Another cunning primate changed the Wiki texts she found,
So apes and chimps evolved from man, not the other way around.
And all religious texts she changed - gave women leading roles.
So female Popes and Mullahs could look after people's souls.

But Hamlet, based at Boston Zoo, deserves his pride of place.
He hacked into the USA's electoral database.
It came as some surprise to the Republicans' grandees
To find that their prime candidate was now a chimpanzee.

A resident of Boston, born and bred in that fair town,
A member of the Tea Party, a speaker of renown,
His CV was impeccable, but could he reunite
The many different factions of the Party of the Right?

The voters of the Right don't really care who they vote FOR.
As long as they're not Democrats, who look out for the poor.
So Hail to the President! Get this country on the move!
A rags to riches story William Shakespeare would approve!

Almost as distressing as my lack of talent with the clarinet, is my inability to get to grips with the Ukulele—just about as simple a string instrument as you can think of ...

I Could Have Learnt the Ukulele!

I could have learnt the ukulele.
I'm sure I would have played it daily.
Those four short strings can hold the key
To music that sounds good to me!

But, my fingers—quite adept at keys
On laptops—are inclined to freeze
When hunting though a uke's four strings
For Dm7s and similar things.

So ever since I had a go
I knew that it could not be so.
No matter which nice chord I plucked
The music simply wouldn't come out right.

The Queanbeyan Bush Poets, who have been incredibly supportive, choose a "theme" for each monthly meeting, by the mysterious process of pointing a finger at a random word on a random page in a book that happens to be lying around. This one frustrated me for a while..........

Damn those Clouds

By vote of the committee, this month's poem's about the clouds,
And according to the rules, plagiarising's not allowed,
But my mind has clouded over—I've a cirrus mental block!
Devoid of inspiration, it's now me against the clock!

I wandered lonely as a—Damn!—That's all been done before!
I've looked at clouds from both sides—Damn! —That's Joni Mitchell's score!
I'd think up something 'new age' style, but even that won't do,
'Cause Django Reinhardt's 'Nuages' has that angle covered too!

And what of Frank Sinatra—always popular with the crowds.
I could p'raps rhyme it his way—he would just send in the clouds!
It's clouds allusions I recall—from fluffy cumuluses.
To dark and stormy nights complete with rainbearing nimbuses,

No match for Wordsworth, you might say, and that I must agree with.
But words like those are fun abusing—playing fast and free with.
I flounder 'round much less in hope than utmost desperation,
Where else am I allowed to turn for poetic inspiration?

It's not as if I'm always blank, sometimes words come out quite freely
And in an ode to clouds, there ought to be some clouds, ideally.
But when it's all been said and done—where poets stand or fall ...
As Joni Mitchell might have said—I really can't rhyme clouds at all.

Australiana

This section offers observations on life as an Aussie—
sometimes from the perspective of a 'Ten Pound Pom', and
sometimes in his adopted style of the Aussie bush ballad.

This effort sort of 'came' to me one day, when I noted that 1988 was being celebrated simultaneously by the Australian government, on the 200th Anniversary of the success of the British sea-borne invasion of Australia, and by the British government on the 400th Anniversary of the failure of the Spanish Armada to invade Britain. I wondered how history would have proceeded if the 'results' of these invasions had been different. It's a long one, but then it's a History of Modern Australia ...

Girtbysea Dreaming

The Beginning –
Our Four Fathers

The story starts in London Town, in 1782.
Sir Humphrey said 'Now listen chaps, I've got great news for you!'
'A wide brown land has just been found, right on the Antipodes,
And your task is to fill it up with British—loads and loads!'

The Four who heard Sir Humphrey were the finest in the land;
And they listened with intent at all the things that Whitehall planned.
Then they loaded up the ships to make the journey 'cross the seas,
With sheep and wheat and cricket balls, and limes and frozen peas.

'This noble task is up to you—the nation bids you well!'
Sir Humphrey said, (although he knew the journey would be Hell).
'200 years from now', he said, 'your names will be quite famous;—
Arthur, Phillip, James the cook, and not forgetting Seamus!'

'And you men here will soon become the Fathers of a Nation!
A task I know you'll do without a moment's hesitation.'
The Four men grinned a bit at this anticipated glory,
Until they got to realise it wasn't all the story!

Continued ...

'To help you in this worthy quest, the Courts have been so bold
As to chain a hundred convicts of each sex down in the hold.
Your job will be to sail the ships down into Bot'ny Bay,
And then to set the convicts free and help them on their way.'

Their downcast eyes betrayed the fact they thought this was remiss.
They smiled again, however, when Sir Humphrey added this:
'And just in case you fear this master plan's a little drab,
The King's agreed to grant you all the land that you can grab.'

So off they sailed, and some time later reached the promised land.
But as they entered Sydney Cove, all wasn't how they'd planned.
Instead of just a vacant lot, with fine, deserted harbours,
They found the locals gathered, tossing shrimps upon their barbies.

Chorus: *Girtbyseans all, let us rejoice, for we are young and free!*
With golden soil and wealth for toil, our land is Girtbysea!

Continued ...

The Wide Brown Land

They set about exploring all the land that they could see,
Anxious not to disappoint His Royal Majesty.
Phillip went to Melbourne, and discovered Aussie Rules,
While Seamus dug for opals and for other kinds of jewels.

Young James was more adventurous, sailing round the coast,
And, of the 204 of them, he prob'ly saw the most.
That how it came to pass he made this great discovery:
'This land's a great big island, and completely Girt by Sea!'

So when he spliced the mainbrace back in Sydney Cove once more,
He shared a beer with Arthur and he told him what he'd saw.
He said 'this place is Girt by Sea, completely filled with land,
And, quite unlike that English stuff, the weather's really grand!'

That's how this land we love acquired its modern appellation,
And how our great Four Fathers came to found this friendly nation.
But while they got the main things right, there's one they overlooked,
And that's the simple fact that all the land was fully booked.

Chorus: *Girtbyseans all, let us rejoice, for we are young and free!*
With golden soil and wealth for toil, our land is Girtbysea!

Continued...(again!).........

Black meets White

So, while the convicts settled in and built old Sydney Town,
A member of the local tribe was watching with a frown.
And, later on, reporting to an inter-tribal forum,
He commented upon the convicts' terrible decorum.

He said 'I heard them talking of a thing called Terra Nullius,
And quickly formed the feeling their intention was to bully us
Into giving up the lifestyle that we Koories all deserve
And shunting us away to some appalling black reserve!'

He said 'I'm going to Sydney Town to try to learn their habits.
The danger is these foreigners will start to breed like rabbits.
The next we'll know is they'll demand Land Title for their village,
And ere too long they'll cross the line to rape and steal and pillage!'

Prophetic thoughts indeed from one unpractised in the art,
But he was mighty Ben Elong, and this was just the start!
Young Ben set off to Sydney Town to infiltrate the foe,
And soon became apprenticed to the blacksmith 'Smokin' Joe'.

At first they failed to notice that his skin was rather brown,
For, after thirty years of smithing, Joe's was darker than his own!
But when he took a shower their curiosity renewed,
And they came to the conclusion 'Ben's been smithing in the nude!'

But soon it came to pass that Ben was able to inform
The members of his tribe about the white men's social norms.
About their great technology, and how they live and breathe,
And how they all get plastered on the night of New Year's Eve.

Chorus: *Girtbyseans all, let us rejoice, etc etc*

Continued...(yet again!).........

The Bogong Parliament

One day up in the Bogong Heights, where all the tribes assemble,
Young Ben described the weapons that had made the convicts tremble.
He said 'They've got these metal tubes that shoot out bits of smoke;
They're weapons of mass destruction and can easily kill a bloke!'

The Bogong moth feast every year provided an occasion
For all the tribal groups to get together as a Nation;
To meet, discuss and clarify the things that really matter;
To socialise and matrimise, and catch the latest chatter.

This Parliament of peoples (as effectively it was)
Negotiated land disputes and passed new tribal laws.
But this year's was a sombre scene, with numerous reports
Of nasty confrontations in which black and white men fought.

Dharruk men and Dharawals were first to lose their lands.
Then to the west, Wiradjri saw the colonists advance.
'If we don't act right now' one said 'and stop this threat at birth,
They could extinguish native rights and spread from here to Perth!

'It's not as easy as you'd think' said Ben Elong at last,
For he'd had a close encounter with a shooting pistol blast.
'They'd easily just wipe us out the minute we advance,
With only spears and boomerangs, we'd never stand a chance!'

'But hear me if you will, because I think I have a plan
That will rid us of the problem and won't even cost a man.'
The elders were astounded at this young man's savoir faire,
So the warriors were assembled and dispatched right then and there.

Chorus: *Girtbyseans all, let us rejoice, etc etc*

Don't worry—we're getting there ... !

The Battle of Sydney Town

The journey down to Sydney Town was filled with trepidation,
All conscious of the fact that it could make or break the nation.
And as they neared the town, all taking care not to be seen,
They heard the New Year revels and 'God Save our King and Queen!'

For the night that Ben had chosen for the battle was tonight,
When the colonising English would be well and truly tight!
But before the fateful hour that poor old Sydney town was sacked,
Young Bennie had to go and do his most heroic act.

As darkness fell, Ben entered Town to kidnap 'Smokin' Joe',
Who had treated him with honour and did not deserve to go.
He found old Joe just halfway through a barrel of home-brew
And whacked him on the forehead with a piece of four-by-two.

He carried Joe back through the bush into the fighters' lair,
And he left him with a Ngarrindjeri woman who was there.
He said 'Take care of Joe, because he really is a mate,
And he's not like all the others, and he don't deserve their fate!'

Then just as Sydney's clocks were chiming in the brave New Year,
Ben's army used the weapon that the Poms had cause to fear!
Their skills with fire were handed down a thousand generations,
And their drunken victims could not cope with midnight conflagrations.

Chorus: *Girtbyseans all, let us rejoice, etc etc*

Continued ...

The Making of our Nation

The consequences of this act were unanticipated,
With repercussions so profound they never since abated.
'Smokin' Joe' brought skills to us which changed our lives entirely,
And an economic outlook that was rated rather highly.

His friendship with the Ngarrindjeri woman also grew,
And the tribe soon welcomed pale skinned kids into the ethnic brew.
They soon became a vital portion of our tribal mix,
Though they didn't get the vote, of course, til 1966.

Girtbysean democracy began at Bogong too,
With a National Assembly house built close to Gundaroo.
Designed by Burley Griffin at the height of his career
With Ben Elong immortalised in marble at the rear.

And now Girtbysea leads the world in Oh so many ways,
We can forgive the indiscretions of those bygone days.
Relations with the English are as good as they can be,
And each year we commemorate their invasion from the sea.

Some Ashes from old Sydney Town, collected in an urn,
Commemorate the night, and all the lessons that were learned.
And this is why we give the Poms' Ambassador a ticket,
To watch the annual replay, when we play pajama cricket!

Chorus: *Girtbyseans all, let us rejoice, for we are young and free!*
With golden soil and wealth for toil, our land is Girtbysea!

The only thing arduous about our migration to Australia was the hold-ups on the flight, but others aren't as lucky as my wife and me !

On Becoming Aussie

Oh gosh—we were excited! The last of the ten pound Poms!
We'd said goodbye to all our friends, and now to our dads and moms.
There were tears as we left, we'd be so far apart,
But we'd kept them a place in our hearts.

The train from home to London—the weight of the suitcases packed;
The thought that we had now committed—there could be no turning back!
There's a rendezvous in London, at seven pm or so,
And a bus full of chat to Heathrow.

And then, the queue for boarding! We're right at the back of the line!
High Commission staff to guide us—telling us we'd be fine.
But it's slow up in front, is something wrong?
Be patient please, it won't be long.

Oh gosh, we were frustrated! The wait seemed to last the whole night.
They gave us food vouchers at nine, and the promise of news of our flight.
And the news came at last, but it wasn't the best,
We were booked a nice room for a rest.

Our sleep was light and fitful. The morning came all too slow.
From our room we saw the runway, and the plane that went to and fro.
The call finally came, we were now on our way!
And now Melbourne was one day away!

The delay was then compounded, our arrival late at night.
Diverted into Sydney, meant another morning flight.
Night at 'Woo-Loo-Moo-Loo', then back on board at eight,
And finally to Melbourne, one day late!

The faithful, met by clerics - 'Let us help you with your gear!'.
For those declared agnostic, just 'your bags are over there!'
And then the ordeal's over; in early springtime heat.
And lots of Aussie friends we'd yet to meet.

The learning curve was tricky—we tried the local beer.
We asked for pints of schooner—that's what they drink round here!
Brightly coloured parrots—assumed that they were pets.
Nearly called for rescue squads and vets!

But now we're nearly natives—even learnt to say 'G'day'!
Drink our stubbies freezing cold; watch Aussie Rules all day.
We soak up the sunshine; we frolic in the sea!
Happy little vegemites are we!

Our neighbours are Iraqis—spent twelve weeks in leaky boats.
Then six years in detention—worth millions of votes!
They're economic migrants—they're by-passing the queue.
But weren't we migrants just like that when we came to Aussie too?

Here's a bit of a surprise for you ...

True Blue What?

Hey, true blue! You know the phrase—as Aussie as meat pies!
We use it to describe a guy who doesn't tell us lies.
We use it as a compliment to people that we find
Are honest folk, and genuine—and importantly, 'our kind'.

But do you know the origins from which these words arise?
Cause I do! And possibly that comes as a surprise
To you - an Aussie, born and bred, to hear these words from me,
A Pommy migrant, long ago, from the town of Coventry.

It isn't hard to see why truth and honesty are linked.
The connection there is evident and really quite succinct.
But what on earth have truth and honesty to do
With anything connected to the primary colour blue?

We use the word whenever someone gets into a fight,
Or when we're feeling miserable—those 'Blues in the Night'!
And blue is for the Waratahs, that Brumbies love to beat,
And then there's Blue the Shearer, whose poetry's so neat!

It turns out that the answer lies buried in the soil
Of my home town, a place where skilful weavers used to toil.
Around the fifteen hundreds—a bit before my time,
When Coventry's great weaving trade was in its lusty prime.

You see, the dye they used in other towns to make their fabrics blue
Was highly prone to fading, more than other colours do.
But Coventry's blue fabrics were renowned across the lands.
Maybe it's the sandstone or the coal on which it stands.

The saying was, in days of old, 'as true as Coventry blue',
And this tradition—modified—comes down to me and you.
Ironic that you think of it as Aussie through and through.
Just as I came from Coventry, this saying came here too!

Australia now prides itself on being 'multicultural, but being from Coventry, we grew up with it!

A Shamrock in his Turban

He was born in September of the 47th year
Of a century scarred by two world wars.
Blue birds again flew over the white cliffs of Dover,
But smoke still rose from burnt cathedral doors.

He grew up midst the ruins of a great industrial town
Whose inventive artisans had built from yore.
But the Nazis bombed the city without any sense of pity,
And the craftsmen and their workshops were no more.

His city was a centre where new technology was born,
From the bicycle to aero engine jets.
If the Phoenix was to rise when the smoke cleared from its eyes,
It would have to face another challenge yet.

Of the millions who died in those years of senseless strife,
The city's workforce was a victim of the war.
And the factories were bereft—there were so few workers left,
So the city sent a call for thousands more.

Those who'd fled from Nazi terror were recruited to the cause,
And the factories were re-manned by Czechs and Poles.
But the city couldn't function 'til the roads at every junction
Had been fixed to fill the legacy of holes.

So he met, while he was growing, all these strangers to the town,
Mostly Irish, who were handy with the pick.
And they shifted heavy loads and they mended bombed out roads,
And their names were always Paddy, Sean or Mick.

As the city and its folk returned to life as best they could,
And new housing built in suburbs out of town,
With high mortgages to pay—and no petrol anyway –
Public transport was the way to get around.

As a schoolkid he remembers meeting different kinds of folk,
Mostly Indians, after training for a week.
And it seemed, on every bus, that the staff was always thus:
The driver was a Hindu, the conductor was a Sikh.

Then, as he became a man, and went out to meet the world,
A Coventry kid—as we Coventrians say,
If the accent on his tongue didn't tell where he belonged,
Then the shamrock in his turban always gave the game away!

Here's another true story ...

The Scents of the Bush

I went for a run, just a few days ago, as I do every day
around seven.
I find that the sights and the sounds of the bush are a
fair proximation to heaven.
I've been running for fitness a few Ks a day, ever since
just a kid at school,
And I run for an hour or so round the bush, about
eight to ten K as a rule.

Being Sunday, there wasn't a need to be rushed, so I
thought I could run a long way,
And I set off determined to finish a loop of a hilly but
nice fourteen K.
The roos and the parrots accompanied me, and the sky
was agreeably blue,
Though, because of the temperature being quite low,
my hands were a similar hue.

I'd run about six K, and finding it tough, but was
stopped by a very strange smell.
It was quite unmistakeably cooking baked beans—an
aroma I know very well.
I'm two kilometres or more from a house, and expected
to see campfire smoke.
But no matter in every direction I looked - no
campfire, no tent and no bloke.

I tried to imagine some other way that baked bean
smells could waft through the trees.
I know all the gumtree aromas quite well, and it wasn't
remotely like these.
Could it be the result of a clumsy attempt to
genetically modify beans?
An Acacia Bakedbeaniana, perhaps, - a tree that is
quite rarely seen?

What else could it be but a bushman's cuisine, with no
doubt a billy of tea.
At that point in my run, a small share of these treats
was a real attraction to me!
But as far as I know, roos and wombats don't cook—I
could rule them right out as a cause.
Yet the smell of baked beans was out there in the bush,
and I never discovered the source/sauce.

What else can you do on an interminable flight to London, when you've heard the
QANTAS 'welcome on board' a thousand times before......

Ol Bitey and the Red

(Welcome on Board *QANTAS*)

The Captain

'Good evening ladies, gentlemen! It's Captain Fisher here.
We're waiting here a moment, 'cause the runway isn't clear.
The weather up above is just as fair as it could be,
And a tailwind should ensure our flight is fast and trouble free.'

'Our route tonight commences with a view of Sydney town.
Those on the left will see the Harbour Bridge and all around.
From there, we cross to Cobar and just east of Uluru,
And then via Bali, Borneo and Phnom Penh city too.'

'Eight hours from now, with even just a modicum of luck,
We'll be gliding down the flight path to the airport at Bangkok.
For passengers who leave us there to take the tourist track,
To match the local time, please put your watches three hours back.'

'I'd like to specially welcome every QANTAS Frequent Flyer,
And patrons of the QANTAS Club, to which we all aspire.
We hope you all enjoy your flight. Our staff are very sure
To treat you well, so you'll come back and fly with us once more.'

'That's all for now—I've just been told to enter takeoff mode,
So we'll taxi to the runway; get this show upon the road.
I'll hand you to the Purser now, to say a few short words,
And then I'll hit the bloody throttle and we'll head off with the birds.'

Continued ... (yes—it's another long one!)

The Purser

'G'day! I'm Bruce McAussie—I'm the Purser for your flight.
We'll be taking off quite shortly, for Bangkok at first tonight;
From there we fly to London, but before we get to go,
I must ask you pay attention to our Safety Video.'

'Our Boeing 747 has ten exits clearly marked,
And lights to guide you to them if we come down in the dark.
If pressure falls, a breathing mask comes from the roof, like so.
(Those with children should inhale first, then give the kids a go).'

'Please keep your seat belts buckled up, while seated in the cabin.
The fastening is simple—merely push the little tab in.
You'll also find a life jacket in case we ditch at sea,
It doesn't happen often—but prepared it's best to be!'

'Hand luggage must be placed above, up in a storage bin,
Or underneath the seat in front if you can fit it in.
Be careful when you get it out, as luggage moves in flight,
And falls on people's heads if you don't pack it nice and tight.'

'Now, smoking's not allowed on this or any QANTAS flight.
And if you do it in the dunnys, you'll be sure to get a fright.
Your seat backs and tray tables must be fixed for take-off now,
Your laptops and your phones switched off. Please let's not have a row!'

'Once we get to cruising speed, there's complimentary drinks
Then comes a three course dinner, and a film—or forty winks.
So settle back, enjoy the food and movies we provide,
And keep your seatbelts on, in case we get a bumpy ride.'

'The crew and I will do our best to serve your every whim,
Though with Fisher at the joystick, I would say our chance is slim!
When last he flew this route, things really didn't go to plan,
While the target was Bangkok, we landed safely in Japan!'

'If Captain Fisher keeps this Boeing in the bloody air,
Your chances of arriving safe are rated pretty fair!
But keep your options open till you disembark at last.
You could find yourself in Bangkok—but it could just be Belfast.'

Keep going ...

And
Me ...

At this, I flushed with anger and expressed my deep dismay
That I should be confronted and endangered in this way.
I waved my arms and protested as loud as I could scream—
Until the flight attendant gently woke me from my dream.

'You've had a busy night', she smiled, 'and held us all in awe
With your talking in your sleep and your ability to snore!'.
I blushed in shame as all my dreadful exploits in the night
Were described by fellow passengers affected on the flight.

The 'air disaster' item that was shown on In-flight news
Must have lingered in my mind—I know it's only an excuse.
I've only got myself to blame—I know it to be so!
But, guys!—I'm only human—so just give a bloke a go!

Back then, on every QANTAS flight, it really was divine
To finish off your dinner with a good old Aussie wine,
Accompanied, of course, by that delicious vintage cheese
That was labeled as 'Ol' Bitey' and was guaranteed to please.

But if you are like me, and prone to nightmares in your sleep,
This is indeed a recipe for trouble very deep.
For peaceful nights—and peaceful flights—before you go to bed,
Avoid the combination of 'Ol' Bitey' and the red!

So QANTAS learned a lesson on that dark and stormy night,
And you won't find 'Ol' Bitey' if you travel on my flight.
For somewhere in their files, my travel record's been endorsed
'N.B. No cheese allowed—This rule must strictly be enforced!'.

The dream of flight's inspired men, from Bleriot to Boeing,
From Kittyhawk to Concorde, Qantas Airways keeps on growing.
And, yes! I had a dream, though not as grand as Luther King's,
But it turned out influential, in the general scheme of things!.

That last one set me wondering about the impacts Aussies have had on the rest of the world, and this one came to me on the long flight from Sydney to Los Angeles one day!

Three Famous Aussies

Some years ago, and quite by chance, three famous Aussies met.
Their lives entwined by quirk of fate on Fox TV News set.
The first was Rupert Murdoch—entrepreneur by trade .
His NewsCorp owned the station—he'd really made the grade.

The next was good Fred Hollows—an eye-surgeon of fame.
To rid the world of blindness was his very worthy aim.
And then the one and only—our own Kylie Minogue,
Whose style of entertainment was everywhere in vogue.

Such contrasting personas—you just cannot stereotype.
The tough old Aussie businessman—the king of headline hype.
The queen of entertainment, with her voice so clear and bright.
And the down-to-earth bush surgeon with the gift restoring sight.

But when the three departed, something strange had taken place.
And Fred's engaging charm now spoke from inside Rupert's face.
And Kylie's nimble fingers ached to heal some person's sight,
And Rupert started singing—giving everyone a fright!

Well, Fred set out to redirect the NewsCorp's slanted views,
And even cured their one-eyed mis-reporting of the news.
And Kylie—cute as ever—went on curing people's sight,
As her eye-opening outfits made her patients see the light.

And that left poor old Rupert—and it really was a farce.
Entrapped in Kylie's body, he could only sell his 'Clars-sifieds'
If I'd,
   If I'd,
      If I'd used the other word just there, it could be misconstrued!
Quite possibly a slander, and at least extremely rude!!
He made a fortune, then, you know, dividing it into squares,
Charging businesses a million each to advertise their wares.

So all three, in their different ways, contribute to mankind.
Fred with good reporting, Kylie's skill—and Rupe's behind!
It goes to show that Aussies have a lot to give the world,
Once their real inner selves have had the chance to be unfurled!

This one is based on, but absolutely not a true record of, a wedding we attended years ago.

The Wedding – the Worst day of his Life!

When Pete and Cathy set the date, the day they would be wed,
They didn't want a church and chose their own backyard instead.
T'would be a civil wedding in which they'd both exchange their vows
In early summer sunshine 'neath the gumtree's spreading boughs.

They searched the Yellow Pages for a Celebrant who'd do,
And set the date and time—December 10th at half past two.
They sent out all the invites, addressed 'To Friends of Cath and Pete',
And Cathy bought a wedding dress that suited her a treat.

Their friends were an eclectic lot, for Cathy was a nurse
And Peter was a bikie, and his friends were something worse!
But even so the stage was set, the barbecues prepared
But then there came the tragic news—the Celebrant was dead!

With only two days left to go these two were in despair,
Til a celebrant named Sheila then agreed to wed the pair.
The circumstances they were in they didn't have a choice,
But on the phone she seemed to have a pleasant enough voice.

The day dawned bright and sunny, and it promised to be hot,
The girls wore summer dresses, which revealed quite a lot.
The blokes just came in T-shirts they'd bought at SummerNats,
And scruffy denim shorts that helped display their bikie tatts.

The alcohol was flowing and the guests were getting high,
As the smell of marihuana slowly drifted to the sky.
It was, in fact, the perfect day for Cath to marry Pete,
And exchanging of the vows would surely make their day complete.

The bride and groom were radiant, in the shade of that great tree
And Sheila, in a low-cut dress, commenced the repartee.
'We're gathered here' and blah blah blah 'love, honour and respect'.
But then the guests were giggling—a response she'd not expect.

A spider, just above her head, the cause of their delight,
Then dropped into her cleavage, giving Sheila quite a fright.
She screamed, and Peter's bikie mates came rushing to her aid
And tattooed hands explored the places where that spider strayed.

Continued ...

The focus of their efforts quickly shifted to her skirt,
As a cry of pain from Sheila made it clear that she'd been hurt.
A spider bite, it seemed, had been incurred inside her briefs,
And the gallant bikie helpers pulled them down to give relief.

But Desperate Dan, who was Pete's best man, exclaimed 'This is a joke—
This Sheila's not a sheila—this sheila is a BLOKE!'
The spider inadvertently had blown poor Sheila's cover,
And bikies aren't traditionally known transvestite lovers.

Well, what came next would even make a seasoned sailor faint!
As numerous creative cures were offered for her plaint!
But Cathy used those nursing skills she'd learnt so long ago -
With her garter as a tourniquet to stem the toxin's flow.

A double dose of Panadol then saved this day of grace,
And the celebrant continued, with the garter firm in place.
The forms were signed and Pete and Cath were legal man and wife,
But Sheila still regards it as the worst day of his life!

A newspaper article prompted this one. I just embellished it a bit!

A Piece of Canvas and a Little Bunch of Keys

Auntie Elsie took a break—she had to get away,
From all the cold of Canberra, to sunny Bateman's Bay.
She rented a nice bayside flat, up on the second floor,
Because it had a balcony—who could ask for more?

Old Cyril was a golfing freak and brought his bag of clubs,
A minute from the golfing greens and close to all the pubs!
He went off to the golf club looking forward to the play,
Leaving Elsie in the shower, getting ready for the day.

The day was warm, and Elsie thought she'd get herself a tan,
With her deckchair on the balcony out of sight of any man.
She thought a tan all over would be nice while she was there,
So without a stitch of clothing, she sat down into the chair.

The seagulls and the pelicans were soaring in the sky,
And Elsie was in heaven as she let the day go by.
But unbeknown to her, her trials were just about to start,
As the canvas in her deckchair quite abruptly fell apart.

Continued ...

Quite suddenly, the bottom literally fell right out the chair,
Leaving Elsie folded up with both her legs up in the air.
She struggled to escape from what was quite a nasty plight,
But every move confirmed that she was stuck there firm and tight.

She called for help, but no-one heard above the seagulls' noise,
And she knew full well that Cyril would be drinking with the boys.
She couldn't hope for rescue—couldn't reach her mobile phone,
She lay there sobbing in the sun—embarrassed and alone.

But Cyril had, by some mischance, left his keys behind,
And wandered back towards the flat not knowing what he'd find.
The doors were locked—he called and called, but Elsie didn't come.
Assuming she was shopping, he just sat there looking glum.

But, getting bored, he wandered to the beach side of the flat,
To sit under the shade—because he didn't have a hat.
And there, above the gulls' loud noise, he heard poor Elsie's call.
He looked up to the balcony - tried to clamber up the wall.

A passer-by soon spotted this, and quickly called the cops.
A burglar in the neighbourhood—he said—he must be stopped!
The pilot of the surf-watch chopper, cruising round, then saw
Poor old Elsie's body there, all crumpled on the floor.

There's been a mishap at the flats, he radioed to base.
Quickly call the cops and get them out here on the case!
The local shock jock then announced to all his talk-back fans,
'Another murder at the Bay, someone should surely hang!'

Then soon the street was full of cops, all bristling with guns.
'Now come down with your hands up! We've got you on the run!'
And next the terrorism squad arrived upon the scene,
Just in case the female victim should turn out to be the Queen!

Four hundred men with pointed guns then aimed at Cyril's head.
He knew that with just one wrong move, he'd probably be dead!
By now completely terrified, he pleaded for his life.
It wasn't helped—it must be said—by the comments from his wife.

For Elsie wasn't in the mood for Cyril and his mates,
And April Fools' jokes definitely something that she hates!
She really thought the cops below were in on Cyril's plan,
And wasn't going to hide the feelings she had for her man!

'You get your arse up here', she cried, 'I'm stuck here in such pain!
This deckchair's got me trapped—I think I'll never stand again!'
Then fifty coppers smashed the door and broke into the flat,
And fifty more grabbed Cyril - held him firmly sprawled out flat.

They strip searched poor old Cyril—quite ironic in a way.
For they covered Elsie up for the reputation of the Bay.
And when they found that no-one actually ever had been harmed,
The cops were glad the threat was gone - alert, but not alarmed!

The situation was resolved. The police force went away.
But Elsie and her beau remember to this very day,
How just a piece of canvas and a little bunch of keys
Can result in situations just as comical as these.

Growing up in mid-20th Century England wasn't always beer and skittles ...

Bathtime for Grandma

We had it tough when I was young, but at least we had four walls.
All six of us in a tiny house, three bedrooms for us all.
Three up, one down, a kitchen, and a freezing outside loo!
There was me and sis, and mum and dad, and gran and grandad too.

Grandma wasn't well, and so had been in bed for weeks,
Upstairs in their back bedroom, with pallid, deathly cheeks.
But one day, feeling better, she called as loudly as she could,
For us to bring the bath up, 'cause a bath would do her good.

So father took the tin bath from off the kitchen wall,
And with the help of my big sister, we lugged it through the hall.
So up our narrow twisted stairs we struggled with this tin,
Then my sister fell back down the steps, and the bath smashed father's shin.

He howled in pain, but we struggled on, our patience wearing thin,
Until we got that bloody bath to the room grandma was in.
So next we had to heat some water on the open grate.
A full bath took twelve buckets, but for grandma, we did eight.

And then we had to lug the water up those twisted stairs.
So dad and I, and he and sis, worked best we could in pairs.
But though we took the greatest care to keep those buckets straight,
The water kept on sloshing out at an alarming rate.

The room got wet, the stairs got wet, dad got in a right foul mood.
I learnt a few new words just then, and some of them quite rude!
But anyway, we filled the bath. Left grandma to her treat.
And stumbled down those twisted stairs to find something to eat.

Well, dad was pleased with me and sis, and gave us each a bun!
But all too soon heard grandma shout 'it's OK now, I'm done!'.
We couldn't tip the water out the window to the street,
So we re-employed the buckets 'til we'd emptied it complete.

We tossed the water out the back, just like a waterfall,
And carted the tin bath back down; hung it back upon the wall.
But when we'd finished we came down, and found the back door wet.
The living room was soaking and yet, and yet ...

This was my family—we made things work. It might seem quaint today.
That's how it was back then, and nowt would e'er get in our way.
A problem like a flooded room was met with 'what's the fuss?'
And we would work it out—that's the way it was with us!

This is almost a true story. Actually it's an amalgamation of a couple of almost true stories.

The Meeting in Melbourne

They wanted me to go to Melbourne—I'd have to fly down for the day.
That meant I'd have to be up at 5 to catch the first flight away.
So, there I was - bleary eyed, checking in around five to six.
Laptop out, mobile phone off, checking out the check-in chicks!

'Sorry', they said, 'your flight's been delayed—shouldn't be much longer though'.
Thank God for the Club—I could do with a brew! Check my emails before we go!
Boarding time's 7:20 now—should still get to Melbourne for 9.
If I'm only a few minutes late for the meeting, they'll understand—that's fine.

The problem, they said, was mechanical—they couldn't get the damned thing to fly.
'Please be patient', they said, 'Text message your friends—if you're late, at least they'll know why!'
So that's what I did, and if push came to shove, I would surely get there for ten.
Any later than that, and there's no point in going. They would have to reschedule it then!

Boarding time's 8:40 now—that means we'd leave Canberra at 9.
A one hour flight and a taxi to town, I'd still make the meeting—that's fine!
The main part of the workshop—where I was to speak—was scheduled from ten until three.
They would just have to wait—it couldn't be helped—they couldn't proceed without me!

The next PA message—'All passengers note—we are SO sorry for this delay.
We're putting you onto the very next flight—arrives in Melbourne midday!'
So another quick text, so they'd know where I am, and we boarded as quick
as we could.
At least I'd be there to express my own views, and the Workshop results would
be good.

Well, we got there! - The taxi went fast as he could, and I got to the meeting at One.
Walked in and sat down, and recovered my breath. Figured out what was now
going on.
While the speakers impressed with their charts and their style, I couldn't relate
to the gist.
I started to wonder, at that point in time, if there could be something I'd missed.

I looked all around, and to my great surprise, there wasn't a soul that I knew.
I whispered just then to the guy on my right, to find out when my bit was due.
'Your topic is what?', he enquired with a smile. I showed him my criminal stats.
In reply, he asked how my figures relate to attempts to control feral cats?

'Feral cats?' I exclaimed! 'Well, I haven't a clue. All my data's related to crime.'
Victoria Police have requested my help to predict future trends over time.
I wasn't aware that cats were a problem that VicPol was trying to fix.'
It was then that he shook his head sadly, and said 'I suspect that THEY met in
Room 6'!

An American friend actually inspired this one, but it's got a real 'Aussie' feel to it!

We Bought a Bush Block

We bought ourselves a bush block—quite near Moruya Heads.
The views were quite spectacular, if you looked past the sheds.
And on it sat a cottage—just big enough for us!
From time to time we'd visit it, as respite from the rush.

Well, one weekend we HAD to go—we'd had it up to here!
We loaded up with nice fresh sheets, and lots of precious beer.
The two hour drive's a nice one, but a means unto an end.
We loved that little house, and felt it loved us like a friend!

It seemed so long since we'd been there—six months, or even more,
And as we got there, all seemed well, til we opened up the door!
Oh boy! The smell! Unbearable! My wife was really sick.
Each horizontal surface had mouse poo—inches thick!

We couldn't stay—drove into town and found a nice motel.
And from the local hardware shop bought stuff to break this spell.
We figured out a stepwise plan. First, clean up all the poo;
Then block up all the places where the pesky mice get through.

With brooms and gloves and facemasks we set about Task 1.
But we still had masses left to do, even when the poo was gone.
We'd disinfected everything—a task we both detest,
Before that smell was truly gone, and we could take a rest!

With aching bones and creaking knees, we thought we'd won the fight.
Too late to drive back into town, we chose to stay the night.
I had a beer, she had a cup of coffee, before sleep,
And we collapsed between the sheets—both of us counting sheep.

I guess our tiredness hid the situation we were in,
As without Task 2's completion, all the mice just came back in!
Stop nibbling my ear, she cried, I need my sleep tonight.
She usually quite likes it, but something wasn't right!

'I never even touched you', I said, 'you must have dreamed!'.
And then she saw the culprit—she leapt out of bed and screamed!
There must have been a thousand of them—maybe even more.
She even trod on three of them, bolting barefoot to the door!

They'd eaten through the coffee bags—were munching on the beans.
And over in the pantry they were feasting on the greens.
With caffeine-fuelled excitement these rodents knew no fear;
Went chomping through our worldly goods; they even drank my beer!

Well, that was that! Abandon ship—return to the motel.
These mice have turned this cottage from a haven to a hell!
So if you're looking for a place that's really, REALLY nice,
Make us an offer—the place is yours—just name your bloody price!

This one is an amalgamation of several 'almost' true stories from when our kids were little!

Camping among the Wineries

Chris and Henry dropped by one day—we'd known them both for years;
Their wine cellar being empty, they'd come up with some ideas.
Their plans involved a camping trip, to see what they could find
To fill that empty cellar with a range of good fine wines.

'Would'ya like to come?', our mates then asked—'the kids would love it too!
Gordon and his wife are in—it'll be a very friendly crew.
We'll fill the cars with camping gear, drive down the old Hume Highway,
And spend the week round Rutherglen, and all those little byways'.

What could we say—a great idea, 'cause in the Riverina.
The wines were great, from Shiraz to the sweet Gewurztraminer
'No tent!', we said, but Henry said 'No problem!' - we could borrow a
Tent from them, and join them at the camping ground at Corowa.

We left work really early, and headed down the road,
Three camper vans in convoy, each one struggling under load.
We aimed to be at Corowa, if we could, by half past eight,
Since pitching tents in darkness is a really awful fate!

The drive went well, the kids were good—we didn't hear a scream!
We played their favourite travel games and bribed them with ice creams.
The camping ground was beautiful, and really picturesque,
So we were all excited as we checked in at the desk.

The first thing that we had to do was build our canvas homes,
And Henry and his brother had those tents that look like domes.
But the one they'd brought for us was of a very different kind;
With poles you had to screw together—a very old design!

We tried to find the corners, since the canvas bits were square,
But every way we fitted them, some bits of it weren't there.
The best we got was three walls up—but then it got too dark.
We found we were attracting quite a crowd from round the park.

'Have you tried this?' someone would say, as if we were obtuse.
We'd try out their suggestion, but it wasn't any use.
From time to time our audience would offer us a drink,
Which made us feel much better, but it didn't help us think!

So as the night wore on, and our construction skills declined,
We farmed the kids out round the park—some folks are really kind!
Some smart-arse then went through the kit as if he were the boss: -
'Your poles are made by Coleman, but the rest is Southern Cross!'

'You haven't got a complete tent—you've just got bits of two!
No wonder that it wouldn't fit—it wasn't meant to do!'
So that was how our week began, disaster from Step One.
Thank heaven for the health effects of Cabernet Sauvignon!

Continued ...

Day 2 ...

We spent the night in sleeping bags, snug in our old VeeDub,
Retrieved the kids at breakfast time, and went to get some grub.
We spent the morning scouring shops to find ourselves a tent,
And settled on a nylon one—the best they could invent!

It proved to be a piece of cake to pitch it in the sand.
The kids were thrilled to find that even they could lend a hand.
Then off we went—at last—to tour the district's fields of vines,
And sampled quite a few of those great Riverina wines.

That evening, round the campfire, it seemed that nothing could go wrong.
And Gordon got his guitar out and led us all in song
A barbie and some local brews then helped us to relax,
And it was prob'ly midnight when we finally hit the sacks.

At 3am—I think it was—the wind came from the west.
It gathered in intensity; the rain then did the rest.
These lightweight tents with skinny pegs, just do not grip wet sand,
Our tent—and us—its contents, rolled away across the land.

Think 'tumble drier action' and you'll know of what I speak.
We tumbled 'cross the campsite till we splashed into the creek.
I struggled with the zip to let the air out of the tent,
But that let in the water, which was never my intent.

So four bedraggled campers had to scramble from the flood,
And crawl back to the car to towel off as best we could.
No sleeping bags for comfort, so we shivered in our seats,
Until the VeeDub's heater could produce a little heat.

Our cornflakes now were soaking wet; our eggs a scrambled mess.
So what we'd have for breakfast was anybody's guess!
Our shoes were in the river, and we'd nothing dry to wear.
We looked at one another in a mood of quiet despair.

Well, being Sunday, some of us would find our way to church,
But after this, we figured that He'd left us in the lurch.
Instead, at 8, we shuffled into All Saints Winery
Dressed only in wet undies—not your normal Sunday finery!

The Winery Shop was keen to sell us nice T-shirts and shorts,
Emblazoned with their logos so you'd know where they were bought.
They served full English breakfast, with some toast and marmalade,
Washed down with a selection of the wines that they had made!

If there's a moral to this story, to learn from our mistakes,
When camping in the wineries, please be careful what you take.
Think twice before you venture out in VeeDub campervans.
Wild weather, wine and wonky tents can ruin all your plans!

One can dream .... with a slight nod to Flanders and Swann!

We Bought Ourselves a Boat

After nearly seventy years of firmly land-locked life,
Retirement to the coast attracted me and my dear wife.
I'd always had ambitions of the ocean-going sort,
But never lived remotely close to any sort of port.

We sold our house and worldly goods; set sail for pastures greener;
And found ourselves a gorgeous place right next to the Marina.
As luck would have it, two weeks after we had settled down,
A huge Aquatic Expo came, with fanfare, to our town.

We had to go—my wife and me—to see what we could find.
Though we couldn't tell the QE2 from the Golden Hind.
We wandered through the Expo, dreaming dreams of what could be,
Past gleaming yachts and tri-marans all ready for the sea.

But million dollar prices put an end to all these dreams.
We had to find a vessel more in keeping with our means!
We thought perhaps a motor boat—we wouldn't have to row,
And with a little motor boat, there's nowhere you can't go.

But on our pensions even that was really quite debateable,
We all but settled then upon a cute two-seat inflatable.
And then the perfect craft for our needs came into sight—
Canadian built - two paddles, storage room, just right!

We could see ourselves as Captain Smith and lovely Pocahontas,
Exploring all the river scenes without a care to taunt us!
'Oooh—that's a lovely kayak', said I, 'and built for two.
But then a voice—with vicious scorn, said 'No—I'm a CANOE!'

I'm a CANOE—no kayak me! I'm also not a yacht!
It's really time you got to know exactly what is what.
Canoes like me are made for work, unlike those kayak thingies!
If you just want to mess about in boats, then buy a dinghy!

But if 'up a lazy river' is the place that you like best,
Buy me—I don't cost a lot—and then forget the rest!
Well chastened by this lecture, we simply stood and stared!
Both thinking of responding, but, in public, neither dared!

To talk to boats, at our age, can signify dementia.
More 'men in white coats' time than riverine adventure!
We paid the price and took it home, and tried it in the creek.
And paddled it like natives in less than half a week.

With tents, supplies and sleeping bags we paddle through the day.
It doesn't have a GPS—but seems to know the way.
At night we sleep beneath the stars, beside the river shore,
With croaking frogs and hooting owls—just who could ask for more?

We often think of city pals, and wonder what we'd do,
If we'd not met, that fateful day, a talkative canoe!

Having recovered from their ordeal at Bateman's Bay, Auntie Elsie and Uncle Cyril venture further afield....

The Night at the Motel

When Auntie Elsie was a girl, she always dreamed she'd go
To see the great Niagara Falls and watch the waters flow.
Uncle Cyril, quite by contrast, couldn't give a damn;
He wouldn't travel further than the limits of the trams.

But, just to please her, he agreed to book a package tour,
At special old age pension rates—that was all they could afford.
The price included airfares, tours, hotel rooms and meals.
It was, Aunt Elsie recognised, a very generous deal.

The flight was uneventful, and mercifully short,
And they were chauffeured straight away to their room at the resort.
Aunt Elsie was impatient to get out to see the sights,
And booked a tour right on the spot, to see the Falls at Night.

Well, off she went, all on her own, while Cyril watched TV.
But three hours later, she returned, as mad as mad could be!
'Just tell me now', she said, enraged, 'exactly what you booked!'
'Show me the papers—NOW', she said, 'I want to have a look'!

Poor Cyril was astonished—he thought he'd done it right.
To give his wife just what she wanted on her birthday night!
'That wasn't Niagara Falls', she said, 'It was just some little creek!
Give those papers over here—I want to have a peek'.

'You silly sod—that's not an 'N'—that there's the letter 'V'!
It's not Niagara Falls at all that you have taken me!
We might as well just stay one night, and go home in the morn'.
That said, she showered, got into bed, and gave an angry yawn.

'At least the motel's nice', she said, 'they've left us bedtime sweets,
Have mine as well', and Cyril did, while pulling up the sheets. '
A pretty blue, but not much taste', said Cyril, half asleep,
But minutes later, passion flared instead of counting sheep.

So now they've booked for next year too, the Honeymooners' Suite,
At special old age pension rates, in their favourite retreat.
It brings back memories every year, of things they wouldn't tell,
Of night-time entertainment at the Viagra Falls Motel.

Queanbeyan is a haven for all sort of people—and wildlife!

Bill and the Kangaroo

It looked a bit incongruous, as they sat there on the hill.
The young adult male kangaroo and a Queanbeyan bloke named Bill.
The setting was idyllic, as these two sat quietly there,
But anyone could see they were a most unlikely pair!

The summer sun was setting, and cicadas sang their song,
But any keen observer would have known something was wrong.
The two sat quietly contemplating, eyes glued to the ground.
For fully twenty minutes neither of them made a sound.

The roo spoke first. 'You won't believe', he said, 'the day I've had.
This morning started normally, at home with mum and dad.
I'm playing with the younger roos, as we do every day,
But mum and dad broke in and said 'It's time you went away!'.

I don't think I upset them, or I said things out of turn,
But mum told me, at two years old, there's much that I must learn.
I must, she said, go bush to learn the adult male's way,
And that was that—I'm on my own—a quite distressing day!

'And what of you?', the roo enquired. And Bill just shook his head.
'It's much the same, I'm thrown out too, and don't know why', he said.
They tossed me out, with nothing more than what I'm wearing now,
Together with my bagpipes, which they said made too much row.

And this is why, as evening falls, around Queanbeyan's bush,
The sound of Billy's bagpipes often breaks the twilight hush.
But you won't hear a snare drum as in Scottish bands they do,
But the rhythmic 'boing, boing, boing' of a young male kangaroo.

My morning runs, and scores of people's dog walks, are threatened by a 1950s-style plan to build a by-pass!

The Bypass

I went for a jog in the bush last week,
down the gully just back of our place.
When just as I'm crossing the beautiful creek,
he and I came to meet face to face.
'Excuse me, sir', were his opening words,
'Do you mind if I ask your advice?
I've observed that you're kind to the fauna and birds,
and you treat the environment nice'.

I stumbled to answer! I wasn't prepared
for a bush kangaroo that could speak.
An event such as this conversation we shared
doesn't happen each day of the week!
'My family and I - indeed all of the creatures
that live in this beautiful land
Are concerned about some undesirable features
the Queanbeyan Council has planned'.

'So they call it a bypass, but a bypass for whom?
It certainly won't bypass us!
Would you like a highway through your living room?
We think the whole project is sus!'
It was clear, the emotion I saw that he seethed with
was justified - right from the start.
To cut out the lungs you rely on to breathe with
is no way to bypass the heart!

No possum or parrot would ever permit
the ring-barking of trees that they live in
So how can it be in the Council's remit?
A mistake that just can't be forgiven!
They say 'Country Living's what makes this town nice,
so how can they plan to destroy it?
There MUST be a 'Plan B' and at half the price,
so isn't it time to deploy it?

It's an engineer's answer to a problem that starts
with the boundaries drawn long ago.
A bypass that went round the westernmost parts
would be clearly the best way to go.
'But then what can we do?' the young kangaroo cried,
'We're all keen to do what we can!'
'No it isn't too late', I quickly replied,
'so listen to my cunning plan'.

'I can get you the forms for the Election in May
when the Councillors fates are decided.
As a candidate you can have plenty to say
on the issues that keep us divided.
With your looks and eloquence the tv will love you.
You'll never be out of the news!
And voters won't rank anybody above you.
They'll all fall into line with your views.'

'And so when you're elected, as no doubt you'll be,
you can make all these plans disappear.
And you and your family and friends will be free
to continue to live without fear!
For the bush is your home, and it's my backyard too,
and to tarmac it all's a disgrace!
Just to give a few truckies a clear run through,
at the cost of destroying the place!'

This one was inspired by a series of wine reviews—sometimes I think they go just a little bit over the top,!

Hunter Valley Water

Hunter Valley water is a miracle of our times,
As good as you will find across the planet.
A wholesome, tasty product of our coastal mountain climes,
And we are proud to bottle it and can it!

Our 'Classic' range is harvested from creeks at dead of night,
When the dust and grime of day is at its least.
Our careful staff scoop bucketfuls that taste exactly right,
And filter out all microscopic beasts!

We recommend our Classic range to go with soups and stews,
Its bouquet will add a spice to any curry.
And this is just exactly what the master chefs will use,
But it's just as good if you are in a hurry!

Our 'Personal Reserve' is now acknowledged as the best,
And is aged for fifteen years in stainless steel.
It actually goes with whatever you ingest,
And you can even drink behind the wheel.

Our 'Sparkling', with its popping cork, and all that creamy foam,
Is the ultimate in luxury for you!!
T'was sprayed on all the winners of last year's Grand Prix in Rome.
It's amazing what some CO_2 can do!

Our Rosé's closely modelled on an Aussie bushman's blend,
Sourced from run-off from our iron roofing's rust
Served up with beef and veggies, is what we recommend.
With the flavours of the western desert dust!

But when you're really looking for that extra special treat,
Our prize-winning Bin Seven is the one!
With hints of highland pastures, and sheep manure and peat,
The aromas linger on, and on, and on!

So raise your glass—so Hunter Valley water's not forgotten,
And hope that global warming is a fraud.
'Cause if it's not, our sources will be well and truly shot, and
We'll have to import water from abroad!

Sport & Recreation

Every Aussie is passionate about sports, and John is no exception........

Another blatant attempt to piggyback on the shoulders of a 'real' poet. For those unfamiliar with the rules of swimming, in a butterfly race, you must touch with both hands at the turns, or be disqualified.

Swimming Matilda

Once a jolly swimmer camped by a billabong,
Under the shade of a coolabah tree,
And he said to his mate as they looked across the billabong
'Looks like about 50 metres to me!'

Chorus: (repeat after each verse)
Swimming, Matilda! Swimming, Matilda!
You'll come a-swimming Matilda with me.
So they stretched and they warmed up, ready for the billabong.
You'll come a-swimming, Matilda, with me!

Up came the starter, mounted on his podium,
'One hundred metres of Butterfly!', said he.
So they stepped to the pool's edge and waited for the gun to fire,
Each looking forward to victory!

Bang went the pistol, startling the wild life;
Off went the swimmers at breakneck speed.
Down in the reed bed, beady eyes searched frantically,
Anticipating a tasty feed!

On sped the swimmers, butterflying beautifully,
Quite unaware of the threat astern.
On sped the croc, doing something like a doggie-paddle,
All swimming hard going into the turn!

Just as the croc thought he saw his opportunity -
Jaws open wide to receive his prey,
The swimmers touched the bank and, dolphin-kicking furiously,
Shot past him going the opposite way!

Croc spun around, his tail thrashing angrily,
Almost a length behind was he!
But he snapped at their heels as they powered to the finish line,
Marked by the roots of a mangrove tree.

Each thought he'd won and, hoping for acknowledgement,
Looked to the Ref quite anxiously;
But the Ref smiled sadly and disqualified the crocodile,
'One handed touch at the turn!', said he.

Elements of truth also in this one. My maternal great grandfather was an accomplished sportsman, and I always loved hearing about him when I was very small. Some of the other elements are also true, including the flood and the cemetery!

Great Granddad's Feat

Great granddad was my hero—the whole town knew his name.
His legendary sporting feats the cause of all this fame.
He captained Queanbeyan rugby—the Mighty Whites of old,
And his bat would out-do Bradman's, if the cricket truth were told.

At tennis, he was brilliant—won at Wimbledon and Kooyong,
Or so great grandma used to say—and she was never wrong!
But of all the stories she would tell that REALLY impressed me,
The greatest was the time he swam from here to Albury.

This mighty feat—two hundred miles—has never been repeated,
And if it was, it's doubtful that his time could be defeated.
Great grandma said he did it in a bit over two days,
And this was years before today's long distance swimming craze!

You'd have to wonder whether he'd have won Olympic gold,
If they'd had a distance swimming race back in those days of old.
So when the Queanbeyan Council opened up their Hall of Fame,
The family made it known that we were keen to add his name.

Of course, they can't rely alone on what great grandma said,
And anyway, for forty years, our great grandma's been dead.
We had to search the archives for some mention of the swim
Before they would consider our request to honour him.

We guessed, for this heroic swim, that he was in his prime,
So we focussed first of all on news reported at the time.
He died in 1956, at the age of seventy three,
So we looked through every Queanbeyan Age from the turn of the Century.

From time to time, we'd find somewhere a reference to him,
In rugby, cricket, tennis—but no mention of the swim!
It seemed so strange, great grandma wouldn't make this story up!
She told it many, many times when I was just a pup!

We asked for help! The archivist agreed to help us look.
And she exclaimed — 'Eureka!' - when she found it in a book!
It seems great grandma might have been creative with the truth,
'Cause great granddad couldn't even swim back then in his youth.

The 'Age' report that finally revealed great granddad's fate
Was about the Queanbeyan River Floods in 1958.
Two years after he had died, God rest him, R.I.P.,
The floods had come and washed away the Queanbeyan cemetery.

Great granddad had indeed arrived on far-off Albury's beach,
Just over two days later, as great grandma used to teach.
It now explains the Mona Lisa smile she always had
When telling me this story, when I was just a lad.

Great granddad's still my hero, 'cause kids need to be inspired,
And—true or false—the story of the swim I never tired.
Little boys need heroes to look up to as they grow,
But it was SHE who gave me one, all those years ago!

I suspect there's not a great deal of truth in this one, but there OUGHT to be!

Great Granddad's Golf Career

I've told you 'bout great granddad, who was brilliant at sport.
Well, some folks say he'd bend the rules if he knew he'd not get caught!
And one day, many years ago, I learnt something of the truth,
When I had a beer, or three maybe, with an old mate from his youth.

The Queanbeyan Golf Club beckoned; it was almost beer-o'clock.
And, leaning on the bar, I met an old grey guy called Jock.
He'd been a member of the Club for over six decades,
And knew my old great grandad when they both played in First Grades.

Oh, yes! He said, Oh, my indeed—yes, he was quite a lad!
I learnt a lot from him, you see—not all of it was bad!
He holds the record here you know, but you won't find his name
Up on the Roll of Honour—the Champions of the game.

All eighteen holes he bettered par, but when his round was o'er
The Club cancelled his membership and showed him out the door!
I was there the day it happened, I was caddy for the man,
Buy me one more beer, son, and I'll tell you what I can!

He was a man of patience, and you'll soon see what I mean,
For he would spend his waking hours in practice on the green.
He mainly practiced little chips, not aiming for the flag,
But aiming it to drop into a little canvas bag.

And all the time, he liked to see the kangaroos come near,
The females brought their joeys, and to him they showed no fear.
Some weeks before the Titles day, for reasons then unknown,
He said he didn't need me, that he'd practice on his own.

But then the great day dawned, and I was with him on the tee.
And he seemed so excited, and it sure rubbed off on me!
The other three teed off, with mighty swings towards the flag,
But he amazed us all and took a chipper from his bag!

He chipped the ball, just twenty feet, aiming for a roo,
It then dropped neatly in her pouch, and she knew what to do!
She hopped away, towards the flag, and joey played his role.
He popped the ball out from the pouch, and threw it in the hole!

A hole in one! Oh, what a start! And you can guess the rest!
All eighteen holes in eighteen shots—my word, he was the best!
Those secret practice sessions with the roos had played their part,
And all those present on the day agreed that it was smart!

But someone then took umbrage - checked up on all the rules,
Declaring your great granddad had played them all for fools!
'No outside force may influence the motion of the ball',
They read out loud, and there it was - your great granddad's downfall!

They kicked him out, but, strange to tell, the rumours carried on.
Some say he played the Circuit in disguise from that day on.
Some say he toured the country in a battered Holden ute,
With a kangaroo and joey, and a chipper in the boot!

Two local villages-Bungendore and Jindabyne-have hosted film-makers in recent years. Bungendore was the scene for part of a film about bushranger Ned Kelly, with-oddly, most people thought-Mick Jagger as Kelly. The murder mystery film 'Jindabyne' was shot around the town itself in 2006. The two villages meet in the rugby Grand Final....

The Grand Final

The great day dawned—the wait nearly o'er—
Grand Final Day at last!
The mighty Mudchooks from Bungendore—
to settle old scores from the past!
The Jindabyne Bushpigs—traditional foes—
in town to spoil the plot.
The players were sober! The paddock was mown!
The atmosphere was hot!

The first half was thrilling—with seven tries each—
the kickers weren't missing a shot.
Both sides were sure—a win's not out of reach—
they were giving it all that they'd got.
With ten minutes to go, the Bushpigs scored again,
the result of a devious rort.
Some guys from the movies—that 'Jindabyne' one—
intervened with some filmgear they'd brought.

From one side of the pitch, they poured rain on the Chooks,
till their scrummaging went all askew.
And their fog machine—a trick right out of the books—
hid the Bushpigs backline from view.
Where they crossed the line was anyone's guess—
the ref made a stab in the dark.
But their kicker then missed, and a sigh of relief
was audible throughout the park.

So with minutes to go, and just five points down,
the Mudchooks played their Ace.
From the film, Ned Kelly, a man of renown,
Mick Jagger then took up his place.
He soared in the lineout, and captured the ball,
quite firmly ensconced in those lips
And he swaggered downfield, with ten seconds to go,
and scored with a flick of his hips.

With the crowd on their feet, and the game almost won,
and only the place-kick to fix,
Jumping Jack gave the Chooks' fans more Satisfaction,
aiming between the two sticks.
Bushpigs sang the blues, while the Chooks ran off
with a win they deserved to enjoy.
But they wouldn't have done it without the help of—
that Pommy Glenrowan boy !

My daughter scored an unorthodox goal in an International waterpolo game ...

The Winning Goal!

After scoring the winner at Ryde
with a backhanded lob from the side,
She revealed that her coach
had described this approach
As one that should NEVER be tried.

At the post-match review with the Press,
one reporter said 'Come now, confess!
If that shot had gone wide,
the game would've been tied'.
But she answered 'Got lucky, I guess!'

And now all the technical chaps
who design waterpoloers' caps
Are working on clobber
for this backhanded lobber;
Rear-view mirrors sewn into the straps.

Her advice for those playing today,
with full-time just seconds away:
If the score's at nine all,
and it's YOU with the ball,
Chuck it over your shoulder—

and PRAY!

Another sporting one ...

Tennis Bawls

The genteel game of tennis holds great memories for me.
Each Wimbledon would bring new players of great ability.
Ken Rosewall was my favourite with his strange contorted serve;
His speed around the court, and his backhand's vicious curve.

I also watched the ladies—like Bueno, Graf and Court,
And lovely Evonne Goolagong—the great ones of the sport.
But nowadays this magic game is stricken by disease;
The women now can't play it without shrieking like banshees.

When Miss Demeanour hits the ball, the wailing never stops.
With screams like that, the wonder is that no-one calls the cops!
Miss Shriekitova's even worse –Whooo—oo—oo—oo—oo—ooooo!
It seems as if the game's main aim is 'who shrieks more than who?'!

What is the point of all this noise? It surely does distract.
Perhaps it's meant to do just that—an unsportsmanly act!
It turns me off—I'm so incensed by this unseemly fuss,
I'm often tempted to exclaim 'You can't be serious!'.

Monnie Seles used to grunt, and players would object!
But shrieks are ten times worse, and must no longer go unchecked.
Just like there's Hawkeye checking if the ball is in or out,
Another gadget could detect the volume of their shout.

And if the decibels exceed some specified degree,
The Umpire should deduct some points - that seems fair to me!
But the best solution I can find to solve this sporting puzzle,
Is to fit repeat offenders with a special sort of muzzle.

It wouldn't look too pretty, but it might at least deter,
And spectators could then focus on the skills that they prefer.
Like serve and volley, lob and slice, and rushing to the net.
And grunting, shrieking players would be the first we would forget.

Social Issues

This section is about the more serious sides of life.
(See next section for the universe and everything).

As social media become ever more octopusian, with tentacles all through our lives ...

Facebook Friends

Will you be my Facebook 'friend', and 'like' me when I tweet?
It really would, I'm sure, make our relationship complete!
We've rarely met, although it seems that we've been friends for years.
I've watched your every exploit, through the laughter and the tears.

I've loved those happy photos of yourself and your two kids,
And grieved for you when times were tough, your life was on the skids.
Your lovely house, right by the bush, I know each nook and cranny,
And how you maxed the mortgage out to cope with dear old granny.

We have so much in common you and I; let's list a few ...
You take your hols in Bali, just like all your best friends do.
You shop at Coles and Woolworths, and bank with the Commonwealth,
And you visit Doctor Foster when you've problems with your health.

Your network's growing bigger now, a quite eclectic lot.
Those jazzy types are interesting—are they still into pot?
The Union guys—you know the ones –who're on the workers' side;
Are you quite sure their friendship isn't something you should hide?

I guess I ought—it's only fair—to introduce myself!
The grandson of George Orwell—his books are on your shelf.
I used to work for ASIO—and I was on your case,
But you never would have thought so, 'cause you never saw my face.

These days it's all so different, thanks to social nets like these,
That allow us all to share our lives with whoever we please.
I miss the phone-taps, eavesdropping, the cloak and dagger set,
But Facebook does it all for me; so much simpler too, and yet ...

I'm still the same Big Brother, making sure that you're O.K.
Right here at your shoulder, should you ever go astray.
I'd like to think that one day you'll see me as your BEST friend.
I'm always here for you, remember, to the bitter END.

If you've ever been monstered by so-called 'Sports Utility Vehicles'—basically 'Yank—tanks' in disguise—then this will resonate with you. If you've bought one— then it might offend— skip this poem!

Cars are just like People

Cars are just like people, with characters like us.
You can even extend the analogy to a truck or to a bus.
But cars are rather special, they are personal, like a pet,
Some are friends for ever, and some you soon forget.

Some are just plain beautiful, with smooth, eye-catching lines,
The E-type Jag, perhaps, might be the best of those designs.
But most cars, just like people, don't stand out for their flair,
Designed for less-discerning types, to get from here to there.

Some have happy faces—Mini-Minors were a treat!
They seemed so pleased to see you when they passed you in the street.
Some are strangely cute—the tough old MGs have this trait,
And driving with the roof down can impress a future mate!

And then there are the muscle cars—V8s and lots of power.
Ferraris and the like that do a hundred miles an hour!
It says a lot about the owners, those that choose to spend
A quarter of a million on a means unto an end.

But what is in the minds of those who buy an SUV?
These ugly, bulky vehicles are anathema to me!
Though built—or so they say—for action on and off the road,
Nine tenths of them are never seen in non-suburban mode.

Aggression is the look that they present to passers-by.
Don't try to overtake ME! I'll smash you if you try!
I'm built to trample everything that might get in my way!
A tank, polluting air and eye; a hulking bird of prey!

Is this the way their owners want themselves to be portrayed?
As rich aggressive nobodies whose lack of taste's displayed?
Is this another triumph of the marketing man's arts?
Or some guy's compensation for his shrinking private parts?

Are these cars symptomatic of the way we all behave?
As if bulked up on steroids, too quick to rant and rave?
I'd like to hear the world all sing in perfect harmonies,
But can that ever happen while we all drive SUVs?

As I actually have a B.Sc.(Econ), I'm qualified to write this one, in praise of the blind stupidity that passes for government policy these days ...

Salute the Economic Rationalist

Throughout the world's great businesses, and in the corner shops,
The economic rationalist is absolutely tops!
Always at our service to improve our way of life,
Minimising waste and driving out industrial strife.

When times are tough, and battlers in the bush can barely live,
The economic rationalist will generously give
Advice on how to shut up shop and move toward the city.
An ounce of economics beats a ton of worthless pity!

And when our business prospects take a tumble for the worst,
The economic rationalist is the one we turn to first.
A systematic sacking of the staff who matter least
Is guaranteed to turn a profit famine into feast.

The principle of 'User Pays' is basic to the creed.
A policy initiative of genius indeed!
So life's little essentials, such as schools, police and health
Are all freely available—pro rata to your wealth.

And infrastructures that we used to take so much for granted
Are so much better private, now the Commies have recanted.
Public transport clogged the streets—made driving such a chore!
But now, they've gone, we're better off—except, perhaps, the poor!

The econ-rat's reduced the load of bureaucratic waste,
So we can fly in unsafe planes if that is to our taste.
And we can die in surgery beds, free of any fear
That overstaffing problems in the wards can interfere.

The elderly, the sick, the poor and dispossessed
Are a burden to economies—a fact you can't contest!
Why should our taxes subsidise a single welfare cheat,
When big business suffers daily in its efforts to compete!

Yes, economic rationalist answers are the best.
Privatise, transnationalise and then downsize the rest.
Eliminate all notions of what's fair and just and true,
Unless they have a dollar value that they can accrue.

For when you see the bottom line there's only one thing counts;
As Fagin said to Oliver, 'In the Bank, some large amounts.'
And as the gap still widens twixt the rich ones and the poor,
One day someone will wake up, and declare at last - **'NO MORE!'**

Lady Mondegreen' never existed, except as a misheard line in the 17th-century ballad, The Bonny Earl O'Moray: 'They hae slain the Earl O' Moray, and laid him on the green'.

The Strange Case of Lady Mondegreen

You know, when detectives look back on their life,
and remember the good and the bad,
It's the STRANGE cases that come straight to mind,
more so than the great times we had.
And one in particular still drives me mad,
and continues to this very day.
It concerned a rich lady, murdered most foul,
whose body was taken away.

I was called to the castle—in Scotland it was—
just an hour or two after dawn.
The caller said clearly TWO deaths had occurred,
and the bodies still lay on the lawn.
'The Earl O' Moray', he said, 'had been slain',
along with his wife, Mondegreen.
But while the Earl's body lay still on the lawn,
the Lady's nowhere to be seen.

I quickly assembled a homicide team,
to examine the scene of the strife.
I assigned my D.I. to the Earl's sad demise,
while I focused on that of his wife.
The case of the Earl was quite quickly resolved,
and the suspect was taken away.
So I interviewed, right to the very last man,
the witnesses there on the day.

Well, stone walls are not rare in these old Scottish lands,
but this was a very strange case!
No witness came forward with anything like
a description of what had took place.
No-one recalled how it happened.
They couldn't remember a thing,
Though I talked to them all, from the scullery maid,
all the way up to the King!

They lied, they dissembled, it was clear as a bell
that they weren't going to tell me the truth!
How poor Lady Mondegreen came to her death,
right there in the fullness of youth.
They denied even seeing her, there on the lawn,
and couldn't remember her face,
So I brought in detectives, forensics and dogs,
and they almost dismantled the place!

Continued ...

But evidence never emerged from the site.
We embarked on a different approach.
A complete search of criminal records showed us
a life led quite b'yond reproach
I then called on the Banks for assistance,
thinking maybe we'd trace her affairs,
But, as fitting her Ladyship's status,
they were probably handled 'downstairs'.

So, just to sum up this sad story,
a double-homicide case at the start,
Turned into a strange missing persons case,
where I.D. theft played a part.
It drove me to drink in frustration,
and I started to visit the bars,
In search, I would say, of new leads to the case,
but mainly to sink a few jars!

Then one night, by chance, I went round for a drink
at a pub called the Dollars and Dimes,
Where a poet was doing what all poets do,
and reciting some verses and rhymes.
I seriously couldn't believe my own ears,
when his verses began to relate
On the Bonnie Young Earl O'Moray -
the details of his terrible fate.

But my interest was soon turned to anger,
as he glossed over all of the facts.
Of our painstaking investigations,
and my team's commendable acts.
So, credit's due where credit's due—
and I think we deserve our share,
For our efforts to find Lady Mondegreen—
the woman who wasn't there!

This one is supposed to be funny, but there's a sting in the tale ...

I Went to the Doctor's

I went to the doctor's a few days ago;
Just routine, but, at my age, you just never know!
'How ARE you?', he cried (for he tended to shout),
I replied 'that's just what I'm here to find out!'.

He peered down my throat, and looked into my eyes,
And he checked that my weight was OK for my size.
Then the blood-pressure monitor measuring stress,
And the stethoscope thingy to check out my chest.

He enquired of my stools, and my daily affairs,
But, as I explained, I prefer comfy chairs.
And as for affairs, he had no right to quiz.
My personal life is no business of his!

'Do you have', he enquired, 'any headaches or pains,
Or shortage of breath, or varicose veins?'
I assured him I didn't, that all was quite fine,
I attribute my health to a taste for red wine.

'I feel pretty good', I remarked, 'for my years,
And, in spite of the decades of blood, sweat and tears,
If I'd known at this age I'd be so fit and strong,
I wouldn't have waited for nearly this long!'

'Then why are you here?', the good doctor then asked,
With a hint of despair, as he put me to task.
'Well, I'm darned if I know', I then had to confess.
'My memory's blank as a gypsy's address'.

'When I booked this appointment, I had it quite clear,
But I just can't remember the reason I'm here.
Perhaps we can schedule a time when you're free,
And I'll try to remember just who I could be ...'

I know a lot of people who would like to see this one happen in real life ...

The
Speaker's Revenge

'Order! Order!! ORDER!!!' the Speaker cried in vain.
You're behaving just like imbeciles—you're driving me insane.
You Members here might well consider what you're here for—
The best interests of Australia—not settling old scores.

These last few hours—you call debate? You wouldn't score a pass
In School Debating 101 - in kindergarten class!
I've had enough of stupid interjections from the back,
And I'll bang some bloody heads together soon, so cut the crap!

True points of order, I'll accept, and deal with as I must,
But these are rare as hens' teeth now. I feel it's quite unjust.
The Opposition's tactics are to stifle real debate,
And entertain the tabloids with the scandals they create.

The use of innuendo, being economic with the truth
Were never so routine in times remembered from my youth.
There used to be some dignified discussion of ideas,
But now there's only insults, ever ringing in my ears.

The Ministers are just as bad, droning on for hours
Betraying all their principles in search of greater powers.
The shock jocks clearly run the game, appealing to the mob,
And if you dare to upset THEM, they'll hound you from your job!

The average person in the street thinks this place is absurd.
One man one vote is meaningless, their voices never heard.
Australians let's NOT rejoice, for we've been put to shame—
Another 'dollarocracy' where influence wins the game.

I now invoke a useful clause from 1392,
It's in the Rules of Parliament, though quite obscure to you.
As Speaker, it's within my powers to send you to the stocks!
So I've had the chippies build a set, made up from English Box.

A copious supply of ripe tomatoes is on hand,
So voters can express their disappointment with your plans.
And genuine democracy will come back to this place
As the ninety nine percenters have the chance to state their case.

It's quite unreasonable for English-speakers to expect everyone else to speak English—but lots of us do just that ... It can be embarrassing!

Why Don't They All Speak English?

Have you been overseas in recent times?
Experiencing different sorts of climes?
How difficult communication is,
And foods that put your tastebuds in a tizz?

What I've been finding specially hard to take
Is the feeble efforts foreign people make
To speak with proper words and clarity.
Why don't they all speak English, just like me?

The French are surely up there with the worst.
You'd think the English language had been cursed!
They're immature from Lille to Carcasson,
Obsessed with wee-wee—every single one!

In Germany and Austria, they tend
To make my wife and me feel just like friends.
But they KNOW her name is Karan, so why WOULD
They always, always, ask 'Is ALICE good?'

The Muscovites are even stranger yet,
And they can't even write the alphabet!
I'm sure it's all the Водка that they drink,
Reducing their capacity to think!

But it's China where things REALLY went astray,
Cause those pictures just don't tell you what to say.
When a hamstring tear became too much for me,
I bought myself a talking dictionary.

I went into a chemist—true, I swear
For 'some tiger for my broken chicken' there!
The guy behind the counter simply laughed,
And I feared that those words made me look daft!

'Jī ròu', he said, means 'muscle' if you write THIS Chinese script,
But it also means a 'chicken', which THESE characters depict!
So, while Tiger Balm is everybody's choice to fix a tear,
My Chinese lessons stopped abruptly in the chemist's there.

I'm giving up—it's really quite absurd.
I'm never going to understand a word!
All foreign tongues will stay a mystery
Why don't they all speak English, just like me?

Chicken   鸡肉

Muscle   肌肉

If modern politics makes you sick, read on ...

My Maiden Speech

If I should stand for Parliament, as I've often thought I should,
It's as an Independent that I think I'd do most good.
I've written down my maiden speech, ready for the day,
In case the local voters ever choose to vote my way!

I thank you, Mr Speaker, for this chance to have my say,
And thank the wise electors for my presence here today.
It's sad, but true, that things have changed, and largely for the worse,
I really can't remember a prognosis more adverse.

It's fair to state the obvious—this country's on the slide.
We're just one giant quarry—a country without pride.
So in this maiden speech, I'll not resile from the facts,
And I'll tell you what I think of what our parliament enacts.

Electors send us here, they think, to represent their views.
But before we even get here, we're told what we can choose.
The options that we're faced with are astonishingly bleak:
You're voting with the Party, or you're finished in a week!

This means, of course, the Party can be sure to get its way
No matter what the merits of what others have to say.
This would, perhaps, be quite OK if we could guarantee
That the interests of the Party and the People should agree.

But the interests of the Party are determined by the rates
Of financial contributions of its members—and their mates.
And the richest of the People never fail to ensure
That the views that they have paid for are encompassed in the law.

This mirrors the relationship that colours all the views
Of the Media proprietors who select what's in the News.
The very same investors who the Party likes to please
Have installed their favourite 'Shock Jocks' on our radios and TVs.

It doesn't take a genius to see where the power lies.
The great commercial interests have their fingers in our pies!
The very multi-nationals and the bankers who're to blame
For this global finance crisis are the ones that run the game!

So here I am, an MP, on the day of my induction!
My slingshot up against their weapons of mass destruction.
My voters sent me here to do a task I will not shirk,
But, to keep the bastards honest will require a bit of work!

I had to use that wonderful Aussie word 'praw', which comes from a traditional Aussie poem about Holy Dan, and this sort of came naturally! I doubt that it is actually a true story— I just made it up.

The Pope Goes to the Dance

Some years ago, in Holy Rome, a strange event took place,
In which the Blessed Mary and the Pope came face to face.
His Holiness, back then, came from Poland - John Paul Two,
And was barely in his sixties, and as fit as me or you.

JP went for a walk one day—he liked to meet his flocks.
Disguised in jeans and T-shirt, and with holy purple socks.
He liked to walk the back-streets—where the pizza parlours thrive,
And the sights and sounds and smells all made him really feel alive.

He found, that day, a brand new place, festooned with neon lights,
The signage said 'The Pearly Gates—Pole Dancing here tonight'.
Well, John Paul was an active man, but rarely had the chance
To relax while at the Vatican—with whom was he to dance?

He also felt a need to reconnect with Polish ways,
Like old-time Polish dances—mazurkas, polonaise.
He booked a place and walked back home. He figured it was right
To let the priests and bishops know that he'd be out that night.

He thought that at The Pearly Gates he should be dressed his best
Just in case Saint Peter should be there to meet the guests.
His purple robes he covered with a simple plastic mac,
Which he discarded only at his seat right at the back.

The show began, and JP was intrigued at what he saw,
As a girl called 'Blessed Mary' took her place up on the floor.
It then became quite clear exactly where she was so Blessed,
As a strange wardrobe malfunction soon exposed her ample breasts.

JP was quite upset at this mammarian display,
And he fiddled with his rosary and quickly knelt to pray.
But the more he praw, the more he saw. And he praw and praw and praw!
Till Blessed Mary danced for him, completely in the raw.

JP felt something stirring—in his heart—and in his pants!
These feelings were so strong that he felt quite compelled to dance.
He took her hand, and literally swept her off her feet,
Till the bouncers intervened and threw him out into the street.

'You filthy creep', they said, 'for dressing up just like the Pope!'
'Don't dare ask for your money back—you haven't got a hope!'
Well! Poor JP was mortified, and quickly fled the place,
But still the Blessed Mary brings a smile onto his face.

Every year brings some new and exciting variant of influenza, often thanks to our farmyard friends—bird flu, swine flu, and whatever they'll think up next.

The Flu

This darn flu has got a hold on me, it will not go away!
I mope around with sniffles the entire night and day.
The nights are worst, it clogs you up, you never get no sleep,
It's full name's Influenza - the French call it La Grippe.

My pocket's full of hankies—wet and soggy every one.
My tummy's full of flu-pills—yet it still keeps hanging on!
I've rubbed in smelly Vaporub all across my chest,
But it's been just as effective as all the bleeding rest!

The coughing fits are worst of all, they leave me feeling weak.
My ribcage aches, my throat's on fire, and there's green stuff down my cheek.
And every time I cough it seems to make me short of breath.
My temperature has gone sky high, I look like I'm near death.

I've been off work a fortnight now, they'll never want me back.
I've used up all my sick leave—so they'll soon give me the sack!
I caught this rotten bug that day I worked til really late,
Trying to do the right thing—helping out a mate.

But when you've got the sniffles, it's just daft to go to work,
Sharing your disease is really acting like a jerk.
Best to stay away from them, and have a few days in,
And try to drown the bloody bugs with large amounts of Gin!

Every Aussie bloke will empathise with this one.......

Demons

A man must face his demons as he lives from day to day.
It starts as soon as he is born, and never goes away.
From infant terrors of the dark to fears of nearing death,
Each demon must be overcome, 'ere he draws another breath

The infant dreams of monsters that devour him as he sleeps,
And then come little sisters, who give every man the creeps.
And soap, and school, and vegies all can stir the fear within.
But a man survives them all—it would be fatal to give in!

The teenage years can make or break a lad, by bringing on
School bullies, pimples, driving tests—the list goes on and on!
And if he can survive all these, the worst is yet to come,
When first his girlfriend takes him home to meet her dad and mum.

Impressing her old man is not as hard as it might sound.
It helps if you enjoy a beer, and shout when it's your round.
And if you know your football and you like his favourite band,
You're on your way with Dad—he'll soon be eating from your hand!

But Mum's a different matter—she has teeth and she can bite!
A dragon breathing fire if you don't treat her daughter right!
No flame in hell can burn as hot as those that emanate
From your beloved's mother if you keep her out too late!

But if you finally win your bride—d'spite all that's gone before,
It's then that you will find that you've acquired a mother-in-law!
Yes—a man must face his demons as he makes his way through life,
But none is quite as scary as the mother of his wife!

Did I mention that I'm no fan of the advertising trades ...?

Steak Knives!

Steak knives—bloody steak knives, clogging up the drawers!
How I hate those adverts—'But wait—there's more!'.
The missis can't resist him—no matter what he's got.
She just phones up and buys it. Completely lost the plot!

We've got saucepans that will never burn, and glasses that won't break,
And genuine Swiss watches—every one of them a fake!
I get drill-sets for my birthdays—I've now got twenty sets!
And each year I get more of them—'cause each year she forgets!

She can't resist a bargain, so the house just overflows
With all those 'special offers'—what we'll do with them who knows!
But recently it's gotten worse—I'm losing lots of sleep.
'Cause she's smitten by those TV ads that say 'I bought a Jeep'!

I don't know what she sees in them—they're ugly yankee trucks,
Worth nothing like the price they want—thirty thousand bucks!
So I went round the dealers where they hook potential buyers,
Armed with sharp new steak knives, to puncture all their tyres.

I'd show these guys who use such lies to advertise their wares,
And don't tell me it's criminal—tell someone who cares!
But wait! There's more! It's tragic how this little story ends.
If you use a 'free-gift' steak knife, the damned thing simply bends!

The power that these advertisers have is plain to see -
To offload shoddy goods onto folk like you and me!
So I've come up with a TV app—kills ads for ever more!
Get yours! Phone this number NOW!! But wait—there's more!

Bureaucratic regulation can be a real pain, but can also present opportunities for change—sometimes with unexpected consequences...

Replacing Rudolph

'A thousand years ago', he said,
'the stars were all so bright
They illuminated everything
as we travelled through the night.
With Dasher and Dancer at the front,
followed by Prancer and Vixen,
Then Comet and Cupid in the third row,
then finally Donner and Blitzen.

Oh, what a team we made back then,
on our annual Christmas spree.
But over the years, the stars grew dimmer
until we could hardly see!
Young Rudolph then to our rescue came—
ah yes! He was only a fawn!
But with his red nose, he lit up the sky—
as if to the job he was born!

Continued ...

There was some dissent, I recall, at the start,
from some of you here today,
But that was quickly forgotten,
and Rudolph was with us to stay!
For centuries now, he has been at the helm,
with commitment that we all admire.
What would we have done without him, eh?
But sadly, it's time to retire.

The years of exertion, the pressures of work,
might have gotten a lesser deer down,
But you, my deer Rudolph, have led us throughout,
with never a hint of a frown.
I'm sure you'd be willing to stay on for ever,
faithfully bearing the brunt,
But the Department of Transport has issued new rules
that prohibit a red light in front!

It's scandalous that your career is cut short
by a bureaucrat's stroke of a pen,
It's required, they said, to align our road rules
with those in the domain of men!
Rudolph, my friend, we all wish you well,
as you enter a new stage of life.
We know you've made plans, including, I'm sure,
that you'll spend some more time with your wife!

As you know, we've been busy recruiting for staff
who are willing to take on this role.
We've interviewed all the best candidates,
in the office up near the North Pole.
We had glow-worms apply, and in some ways they're good,
but they simply can't race through the sky.
And a cheetah, while fast, would upset all the deer,
with that predator gleam in his eye!

We finally settled on someone who came
with credentials we couldn't resist,
Like you, she was born with the skills and physique
that matched our exhaustive checklist.
Like yours, her proboscis lights up in the dark,
but hers is a brilliant white.
She has full Motor Registry certification,
for sleigh rides in daytime or night.

She'll bring one new skill to our Christmas Eve runs,
that even old Rudolph can't match,
If there's not enough room for the toys in the sleigh,
she can fit the excess in her pouch!
So, Ruby, the White Nosed Kangaroo,
please step up and meet my great team.
You're now our new leader, to show us the way,
fulfilling all good kiddies' dreams!'

No billionaires were hurt in the production of this one, and no particular individuals came to mind...

Black is the Colour

Black is the colour of my true love's Rolls,
proceeds of his financial goals.
He might be old and past his best,
but who can match his treasure chest?
Being married to a billionaire—What's wrong with that?
Why should I care?

Our different ages, some would take as evidence I'm on the make.
But nought is further from the truth,
and his great age and my great youth
Are balanced by the difference in his wrinkled,
and my flawless, skin.
I revel in the luxuries, that will be mine
though now are his.

And when I'm lying in his arms, my thoughts are full of tropics, palms
And spacious villas on the beach.
All of this - within my reach!
I love his young accountant's smiles,
holidaying in the Cayman Isles.
All tax-free haven business trips,
complete with secret skinny dips!

We two would make a pretty pair. What's wrong with having an affair?
P'haps this is where my future lies,
as soon as my old husband dies.
I'll play the role of loving wife,
to set the scene for future life.
A marriage of convenience comes
with substantial recompense!

Why do you stare and look askance? You'd do it if you had the chance!
Don't hold back on your wedding night.
Invest it while you've got it! Right?
A few short years 'tween rich men's sheets
result in rather large receipts.
A post-coital heart attack
can put your future plans on track.

No foul play would they detect, and you would never be suspect.
Just make sure that he has his fling.
You'll soon inherit all that bling!
Another way to lose your pet
is to tamper with his private jet.
A sweet soirée with the engineer
might be all that's needed here.

The last thing that you want, of course, is to lose it all in a divorce.
Divorce is messy—there's no doubt,
and judges might just leave you out.
A settlement is nowhere near
as lucrative as shedding tears
In widow's black—
the mourner's choice—
Goes nicely with a black Rolls Royce.

I think I may have mentioned that I don't like marketing—
here's an example of why!

Only Needed Milk!

The missis took a break last week, and left me on my own.
She left the pantry well stocked up, so I had no cause to moan.
The fridge was full of beers, and she had ironed all my shirts,
So things went well for several days, but then turned for the worst.

It seemed like such a simple thing, at least it did to me,
To put a bit of milk into my breakfast cup of tea!
But I must have left the milk jug out, 'cause next day, if you please!
I poured the milk into the cup, and out came cottage cheese!

It really didn't taste too good. But how hard can it be
To venture down the shops and get some milk for morning tea?
I never do much shopping, 'cause the wife sees to all that,
But still, I thought, I'd just pop down—be back in minutes flat!

It wasn't quite as quick as that. As I said just now to you,
The wife does all the shopping, and I hadn't got a clue!
I tried the haberdashery, and they were quite polite.
And showed me to the big shop, round the corner to the right.

I found the dairy shelves, no sweat, but then I got a scare,
With forty different brands of milk up on the shelving there.
There was skimmed, organic, lactose free, low fat and high omega.
There was some from Gippsland, some from Dubbo, and lots of it from Bega.

I asked the staff—'I just want milk!'. They laughed and left me to it.
So I looked in vain for something that would help me puzzle through it!
Is soymilk what the missis buys, or milk that's been condensed?
Homogenised or pasteurized? It didn't make no sense!

I just gave up—it seemed too hard—and found a little place
With breakfast on the menu and at last a smiling face!
A crispy bit of bacon and an egg or two would be
A perfect way to rescue me from this catastrophe!

She said she'd be delighted to, she was such a charming lass!
How do you like your eggs today, she very sweetly asked,
Over easy, sunny side up, soft boiled, poached or hard?
And cooked in butter, margerine, or olive oil or lard?

An omelette, or frittata? Fried or scrambled, hens or goose?
At this point, quite confused, I made some meaningless excuse.
Oh, sorry, love, I've changed my mind. I'll have some tea instead.
I thought that there could be no risk, but this is what she said:

'Green tea, black tea, herbal tea, oolong or rooibos?'
At this point I was speechless, and was really getting cross!
What happened to the good old days when eggs and milk and tea
Were simple foods we knew and loved, like they're supposed to be!

I just cracked up, I went berserk. Went screaming through the Mall!
I must have been quite scary, as they gave the cops a call.
The missis bailed me out, but now there's one thing we agree.
It's she that does the shopping when we need milk for our tea.

I've never been able to work out why Aussies prefer their beer to taste of nothing but 'cold'. One of the major brewers even claims their stuff is 'made from beer', so why didn't they stop when they were ahead?

S(h)inging the Brews

Not far away, I think I'd say 'bout fifteen K from here,
I found a place where you can choose your recipe for beer!
Well, as you know I'm no real fan of the cold and tasteless kind
That's served up by big brewers, so I thought I'd try to find
A recipe that suited me—to hell with all the rest!
I'd be like Frank Sinatra and do it my way—that's the best!

When I perused the various brews, to suit these tastes of mine,
The one I wanted most of all was labelled 'Barley Wine'.
It's not a real wine at all, but a real strong Scottish Ale.
A malty, hoppy beer that puts the others in the pale.
The double-dose of malt and hops is vital to the flavour,
And guarantees a brew that any connoisseur would savour.

The barley grains and hoppy strains go in with the malty goo,
And boil in a giant vat to create this mighty brew.
Almost an hour goes by before the yeast itself goes in,
And that's the point at which the fermentation can begin.
Then three weeks later—if all is well—the bottling can start,
And—truth to tell—this really is the most exciting part.

The bottles must be free from dust and washed before they're filled.
The beer is poured with tender care so nothing's ever spilled.
Of course, it's fair to test the brew from time to time, to see
If it meets your expectations in terms of quality.
My rule of thumb is—fill up six and test each seventh drop.
That way you'll know your brew is good, from the bottom to the top!

In my experience, bottling beer's the way to spend the day.
The seventh beer goes down the hatch, and sends the blues away.
The fourteenth beer will reinforce those feelings of goodwill,
And number twenty one will make you feel better still.
Twenty eight is maybe where I ought to draw the line,
But—seriously—this stuff is good—a beer that suits me fine!

Some time later............

That's fifty now—I don't know how I missed out forty nine! (Swig!)
I used to think mathematics was a special skill of mine!
So ninety four to go, in all, and only half past three.
I should be done by five o'clock, and be back home for tea.
Now where was I? It's shixty shix? Does that divide by sheven?
No - not at all—'cause shixty shix is just shix times eleven.

Some time even later............

Sho when's my next one? Must be shoon—ah—number sheventy!
This beer's SHO good—exshibiting a fine (hic!) complexshity.
It lingersh on the palate; itsh (hic) bouquet is quite exshquishite,
I'm going to make shome more of thish when nexsht I come to vishit!
But, mushn't shtop - more bottlesh left, and almosht half way
through it!
Itsh tricky now the bottlesh move, but shomeone's got to do it!

'Roooooooooll out the Barrel ...'

Science and Philosophy

Big Bangs, Evolution versus Creationism, the End of the World—and lots of things in between!

Evolution has a way of putting things in perspective!

Reflections on Being the First Living Creature.

I think I'm alive!! I'm not sure, 'cause, you see,
There's never been something remotely like me!
I'm not like the rocks or the sea or the sky.
I'm a multi-celled creature that one day might fly!

By some stroke of luck, DNA's in my cells.
One day I'll grow organs for sounds and for smells.
One day I'll grow eyes, and I'll see the whole world,
And I'll have a brain, once Evolution's unfurled.

It's exciting to think that I am the first,
And though I'm the simplest, I won't be the worst!
I guess that there'll be some black sheep in the breed.
Descendants like T-Rex are ones you don't need!

My sons and my daughters, and their offspring too,
Might be a giraffe, or a cute kangaroo.
And those monkeys—my god! Evolution's mistake!
If they ever walk upright, the trouble they'll make!

But wait just a minute! These thoughts are just great,
But how in this world do I procreate?
It's got to start somewhere—it must be with me,
But I'm just a blob tossed around in the sea.

Don't know if I'm Adam; don't know if I'm Eve.
Or if there's a God—don't know what to believe!
I think, so I am, but what happens next?
I have to confess I'm completely perplexed!

I suppose if I try to explore what's around,
There might be another like me to be found.
Together, we'd somehow work out how to mate.
The first in Creation to then procreate!

They'd write love-songs about us—Romeo 'n Juliet!
I can see it all now, though we've not even met!
But what if there are no more blobs just like me?
How can I fulfil what is my destiny?

Should I just sub-divide? Is that all there is to it?
If there's no other choice, then I'd better just do it!
At least in this way, as a mum and a dad,
Our kids would have parents that I never had.

It's a start—a beginning—a new life, I suppose,
But not as romantic as I would have chose.
But a guy's gotta do what a guy's gotta do,
So watch me as I divide into two!

A colleague's birthday prompted this one... You need to know a bit of maths!

Old Programmers Never Die...

So, you're 50 years old, and life's taking its toll;
The silver threads more than outnumber the gold!
But there's no need for panic—no need to feel sad,
    Mathematics can show that it isn't so bad.

Five Zero may seem like a zillion to you,
But in Octal it's worse—you'd be aged 62.
And in Binary you'd be quite the oldest of men—
One hundred and ten thousand years, and ten!

But computers are smart—while they use Binary codes
For digital storage and file downloads,
When talking to humans, that isn't the norm:-
Their messages take Hexadecimal form.

So don't let them say you've one foot in the grave,
And take heart from the way that Hex numbers behave.
For in sweet base sixteen lies some good news for you:-
Happy Birthday, old fellow—now you're just 32!

Or, mathematically, $50_{10} = 62_8 = 110010_2 = 32_{16}$

The 21st Century exploration of Mars—a new 'Terra Nullius' - bears some similarities to the exploration of Australia hundreds of years earlier

Take Me
to
Your Leader

'Take me to your leader', said the Martian to the Queen.
'I AM the leader', she replied, 'Whatever do you mean?'
The Martian—fumbling for his words—(he meant no disrespect!)
Said 'I'm sorry, dear old lady, but you're not what I expect!'

'Not what you expect, I'm sure!' Her Majesty replied.
'But don't stand out there on the steps—you'd better come inside!'
'It's rare for me to entertain a visitor from Space,
In fact, I can't recall a Martian ever in the place!'

'You take a seat– I'll make some tea—and tell me how you've been.
You must have had an awful trip—your face has gone quite green!
Is Mars still in the Commonwealth? I really can't recall.
In fact, I don't remember if they ever joined at all'

'I've come in peace', the Martian said, 'My people don't want war.
But we're concerned to find out what you guys are looking for!
We fear the British Empire is attempting to expand,
Through all this exploration taking place on Martian land'.

Continued ...

'The day's long gone', the Monarch sighed, 'when Britannia ruled the waves.
It's Elizabeth the First you want—we don't do that these days!'
'So who's in charge?' the Martian asked. The Queen replied 'The Yanks!!!
You'd best talk to the White House—or they'll send in the tanks!'.

'I'll get him now on Skype for you—he's always on the line.
'Hello, Barack—it's Lizzie—how's Michelle?—yes, Philip's fine!
I've got a nice young Martian here, he wants to have a chat
About your Mars Explorer plans, and what they're aiming at.'

'I'll put him on—byebye for now. Here's our Martian friend.'
But all this royal politeness quite abruptly was to end!
'We want him here', the White House said, in no uncertain terms!
'He represents the rebel side, and he may have lethal germs!'

'He's double-parked his space-ship, which may well be nuclear armed,
Please tell him to surrender now, and he will not be harmed.
We want him extradited to face justice in our courts.
The Military ones, as he's a combatant of sorts.'

'The CIA will pick him up—don't worry 'bout the cost.
And they'll require his space ship too—evidence must not be lost!
Guantanamo's quite empty now—accommodation's great!
The sand's quite red—he'll feel at home—while we decide his fate'.

'We can't have Martians running round as if they owned the place.
If innocent, we'll set him free to go back into Space.
If guilty, then he'll prob'ly hang—that's if he's got a neck'.
The Queen—while quite upset at this—agreed to double check.

On hearing this, the Martian turned and bolted for the door.
A flash of light, a thunderclap, and he was there no more!
His double-parked space ship simply vanished to thin air.
It was as if the pair of them were never ever there!

The White House—feeling thwarted—imposed trade sanctions on Mars,
And banned the importation of those well-known chocolate bars.
So once again the USA's hardline stance won the war,
And double-parking Martians pose a threat to us no more!

Has technology gone as far as it can—or maybe further than it should have??

Logging Out

The residents of a retirement home just
love to reminisce.
They talk about the old days as if they were
full of bliss,
And they talk about their grandkids, and how well they're
doing at school,
But 'things ain't what they used to be' is their favourite,
as a rule!

Picture the home for retired computers:
- a be-wrinkled IBM
Has a Hewlett Packard bailed up in the lounge—
let's listen in to them!
'In my day—when IBM ruled the world—I was
bigger than Ben Hur!
My air-conditioning units alone would stretch from
here to there!

My magnetic tape units—20 or so—were in action
at my beck and call,
So the pay calculations were EXACTly right—I was always so
proud of them all!
International Business Machines—that was us—we served our
owners well.
Did the work of five hundred payroll clerks—and printed the pay-
slips as well!'

'Big deal!' said the HP, 'So all you achieved was to usurp the jobs of
those staff!
My role was much grander—in research, I was, doing linear
regressions and graphs.
I worked on designs for space rockets and things—stuff that
previously couldn't be done!'
At two hundred and ten calculations an hour, my work rate was
second to none!'

The one thing the two of them did agree on was that things had
gone badly awry.
'We thought we were movers and shakers back then, and our hopes
for the future were high!
Our kids were much faster and cleverer than us, and could fit on
the top of a desk,
But the grandkids—so spoilt—so vacuous—so small—the science
has gone quite beresk!'

'You'd think', said the HP, 'with those processing speeds, they could
set themselves more worthwhile tasks!
Like solving the world's finance crises—surely that
isn't too much to ask?
They could, p'raps, eradicate hunger, or find out
what's killing the frogs;
Instead all they do is Twitter, and iTunes and Facebook,
and blogs!'

Continued ...

'What use is it all?', IBM sighed at last, as he sipped at his
tonic and gin.
'Things are not what they used to be, and that's a fact—just look at
the state that we're in!
Every kid's got a laptop, an iPad, a phone—each a billion times
cleverer than us,
But the world's not one tiny bit better for that—in fact, you could
argue, it's worse!'

'Charles Babbage, Alan Turing, Herman Hollerith and all—the
great men from whose minds we came,
Must turn in their graves to see what we've become—just a toy that
enfeebles the brain!
Come on over, old timer, and let's end it now—just give me
one last big hug!
We're too old for this world, so when I say the word, let us finally
pull out the plug!

It's just as well I didn't become a doctor or a surgeon—I have all sorts of trouble identifying different body parts!

Oh! Why do we have Kneecaps?

Oh! Why do we have kneecaps?—they're of precious little use.
They must have some real purpose, though to me it's quite abstruse.
We don't have elbow-caps at all—that causes us no harm,
So why have caps upon our legs but not upon our arms?

Why is our bottom half-way up? It's a mystery to me.
How strangely named—this misplaced part of our anatomy.
Consulting my thesaurus, to see what wisdom it contains,
I find that 'bottom' means 'the foot', so I'm baffled yet again!

What happens to our laps whenever we decide to stand?
Where do they go to? Here again, I'll never understand!
They're really quite perceptive, when you come to think of it.
And always reappear the very moment when we sit!

Why was it, in the sixties, that the colour of our skin,
And the length of our hair defined the state that we were in?
But in our sixties, sagging skin and heads no longer crowned,
These attributes seem best described the other way around!

Continued ...

Why is it that our noses run, and why do our feet smell?
It should be round the other way—as far as I can tell.
The human body's many parts all seem to be misplaced,
As if it were—I hate to say—designed in too much haste!

Our bodies were, the Bible says, designed for us by God.
If that's the case, it seems to me, these faults are rather odd.
What kind of skills did God possess to fit him for this task?
What training did he have? A question someone has to ask!

A schools department architect, perhaps, who could have made
Mistakes that would be typical of others in his trade.
For just who else could ever find as silly a thing to do as
To set the playground down between the outlets of the sewers?

If you've spent as many nights as I have in motel rooms, this debate might seem familiar...

Soap

versus

Gravity

The Romans gave us baths, they say, two thousand years ago.
Cleopatra bathed in asses' milk, or so the stories go!
Archimedes found displacement while relaxing in the tub,
And Einstein had his relatives to give his back a scrub.

Yes, baths have been a part of life for many, many years.
I remember as a toddler how the soap got in my ears.
But later on I grew to like that creamy soap's caress.
That sodium stearate magic touch that makes you feel so fresh.

But here in Oz, we stand up while we take a cleansing shower.
It uses less hot water though you might stay there for hours.
It takes some getting used to, 'specially when you wash your feet,
Pirouetting like a dancer, on one leg, but not as neat!

But nowadays it's hard to find a proper cake of soap,
And shower gel is all the rage. I s'pose I'll have to cope!
But is it really sensible to use this oily gunk,
That's specifically designed to slither quickly down your trunk?

The problem is—it seems to me—that gel is not designed
To stay upon those body parts to which it was consigned.
It slithers down until it gets entangled in your loins,
And works just like shampoo down there, but really what's the point?

The manufacturers of this stuff would like us to believe
It's just a better way to wash, but that won't wash with me!
It's just a hoax, all marketing, and naught but gimmickry,
It might well work in outer space, but not with gravity!

*It seems that not everybody has the same trouble as me, including my talented,
though clearly misguided, daughter-in-law, Renée...*

Renée's Response!

In answer to the issue of the slippery soap debate
I'd like to offer some advice before it's just too late.
If you find yourself confronted with a bottle of the gel
When visiting with relatives or at a nice motel,

The thing you must remember is it's really all technique
Find a lather making implement and your cleanliness will peak.
Grab yourself a loofah; a flannel will even do.
And voila! Foamy lather - not merely loin shampoo.

The danger of the caked kind - simplicity aside—
Is how to safely grasp it. All methods have been tried.
I'm sure you've heard it said before - people find it hard to cope!
The ardent warning ringing true - Careful! Don't drop the soap!

But, I'm determined to have the last word— it's MY book, for heaven's sake

Response to Renée's Response!!

This really seems to prove the point that I have tried to make.
For gravity poses problems for either gel or cake!
But hunting round for loofahs seems a massive waste of time,
When your primary purpose is to rid yourself of grime!

And cake-soap has attributes you really can't ignore,
Since, unlike gel, it can rebound right back off the floor!
And if you are so clumsy as to always drop your soap,
The markets sell a range of soaps that dangle from a rope!

My case is closed—the issue's won. I've let you have your say!
A cake of soap's superior in every single way!

Recent scientific breakthroughs have confirmed Einstein's theories about the beginnings of the Universe—but what happened before that?

In the Beginning

We humans thirst for knowledge—well, some of us, at least!
From white-coat men of science to the mystics of the East.
We observe what is around us, make some sense of what we see.
A prime example being Einstein's Relativity.

Albert Einstein was a genius, and his theories shed new light
On how the universe was formed—the Big Bang in the night!
Who would have thought, for instance, that a moving clock ticks slow,
And gravity can change the way we see a light beam's glow.

But subsequently each and every one of these ideas
Has been proven to be fact—the world is not as it appears!
Creationists, it must be said, still won't admit he's right,
And quote from ancient documents to prove that God is Light.

But scientific method is remorseless in its quest,
And labs all round the world compete to find out who's the best.
Just picture those great scientists, how excited would they be
To find themselves observing waves of Big Bang gravity!

A fraction of a second after that Big Bang took place,
The universe inflated at a meteoric pace.
Gravitation was created that has rippled through to us.
The evidence has now become quite unambiguous.

But what, enquiring minds will ask, preceded these events?
Debate about this question is exceedingly intense.
A Nobel Prize awaits the one that solves the mystery
Of what provoked that key event in cosmic history.

Now confident that they'd find out what really had occurred,
With bated breath, they played the tape, and this is what they heard...
A still small voice says, through the phones, not loud, but very clear,
'I wonder what will happen if I press this button here...

BANG!!!!!!!!!!

If you're from a pre-technological age, this will seem familiar ...

Predictive Text Blues

I have a problem—I'm NOT alone— 'Predictive Text'
on my mobile phone.
I tried it once—it made no sense. I vowed that I'd
not use it thence.

I watched the News—they've used it too.
And, Oh! The shame that then ensues!
Predictive text works fine for some,
but when it's wrong it's really dumb.

I heard one night the newsman say
there'd been 'a violent—soufflé'!
A 'scuffle' seems to've been the word,
but 'type ahead' made it absurd!

And in the football news we heard,
again, a typo in the words...
'Tim Cahill scored a superb goat'!
No doubt the words froze in his throat!

And on the Tour de France one day,
I heard the poor newsreader say....
'Cadel Evans had a lengthy leak'.
Had he been in the pub all week?

In entertainment news they said
that 'Elvis Parsley' wasn't dead!
Though he might have left the room,
that wasn't cause for doom and gloom!

The weather news was even worse—
predictive text had left its curse.
A 'froggy' day in London Town?
Would that mean lots of French around?

Predictive text could start a war,
used by the Diplomatic Corps!
The word 'ally' would mean a friend,
but 'a lie' would mean the end

Of treaties that keep global peace,
and threat of war would soon increase!
Between you, me, and these four walls,
I'd have him strung up by - nightfall,

The guy whose invention has me vexed ...

The one who invented—

MOBILE PHONES! SOCIAL MEDIA! ALL OF IT!!

Is there an afterlife? Do we come back as different creatures? I doubt it very much, but it's fun to speculate!

The Bug

If I were a bug, I'd like to be
The sort that dangles from a tree.
I'd wait and wait til someone came
Then drop, and play my little game.

I'd wander through her well-combed hair
And take a bite just here and there
And when she'd raise her hand to scratch
I'd move on to another patch.

A few more times like this is sure
To send her looking for a cure.
But I'd be several steps ahead,
And lurking in my victim's bed!

As bedtime comes, she'd tuck me in
Right next to her attractive skin.
A victim primed for me to bite!
A tempting feast that lasts all night

When she awakes, she'll strip the bed
Again I'd be one step ahead.
She'll wash the sheets while I stand by
And then she'll hang them out to dry.

And as they flutter in the breeze
I'll jump right back into the trees.
Then, I'd wait and wait til someone came
Then drop, and play my little game ...

Oh, what a lifestyle this would be!
It seems like paradise to me!
Good food, a cosy bed each night.
Would you not say 'a bug's delight'?

Is mankind created in the image of God? Is there a 'Chosen Race' amongst us?
Have these questions already been asked—and answered—before?

The End

It's nothing to fret about, baby', she said
As we watched the great fireballs streak overhead.
'It will be as He wills it, in these final days,
Then this Earth will become a more peaceable place'.

For the good Lord Creator, in whose image we're made,
Has foretold of this time, so be not afraid.
For the dinosaurs, true—it's the end of the world,
But, for us, the Creator's great plan is unfurled'.

'These fireballs from Heaven are His way to tell
The bad dinosaur creatures that they'll go to Hell.
'They won't hurt us—be brave—the darkness will end,
And our lands and our oceans will be on the mend'.

'Snuggle down in your nest, till the firestorm stops,
And dream of the days when triceratops
And T-Rex are no longer a threat to our lives,
And the Lord's chosen creatures—that's us - will survive'.

'The Creator's determined the future of things.
We're His chosen creatures—that's why we have wings!
While the dinosaurs die in the hellfires down here,
We birds will ascend to His Heaven up there.'

Mother's words seemed to comfort me, at least for a while,
And I lay back, relieved by the warmth of her smile.
Was it true that the reason the Lord gave us wings
Was to rise up to Heaven to become Queens and Kings?

How lucky for me, to have been born a bird.
To inherit the Earth by the Creator's Word.
What wouldn't I give to hear the Lord speak,
And just to be there when He opens His beak!

'I imagined, just then, how the heavenly throng
Would thrill to the sound of a million birds' song!
And I thanked the Creator, for under His Plan,
The last laugh will be had by
                                    my
                                        Kookaburra
                                                    clan!

I told you it was 'The End'!

www.ingramcontent.com/pod-product-compliance
Lightning Source LLC
LaVergne TN
LVHW021133080426
835509LV00010B/1339